WHAT PEOPLE ARE SAYING

"As I read her words I cried, the sincere expressions of the deepest heart-cries of my lover, my friend, my wife of nearly 20 years being poured out on these pages. Elisabet is my hero. She has loved her Jesus like no one I've ever known. I pray that her exposition of this Song will stir your heart to love Him more, as her life has always stirred me to understand and embrace His devotion as the Lover of my soul."

— Robert Fountain, Senior Pastor, Calvary Chapel Miami Beach

"Elisabet Fountain has brought a fresh and creative look to the Song of Songs. Her insights are spiritually probing, practically useful and utterly inspiring. My vote is thumbs up!"
— J. Bruce Sofia, M. Ed., D. D., Author and Speaker, Founder and Senior Pastor, Gloucester County Community Church

"Thank you for writing this book. Thank you for a manual that truly guides and lights the way to Him alone who gives one the tools to manage where one can not. How-to books don't work in this life of being a disciple. Only HE can truly fill every gap. Thank you for being faithful to hear the story He has given you to share."

— Erika Piagetti, www.ftcbrazil.org

"I read very fast, I can finish a 200pg book in a couple of hours, and initially I planned to whip through yours and get straight back to you, however almost immediately that I started it I found myself wanting to go slowly and reread pages two or three times. And I wanted no distractions at all so I have found myself carrying it everywhere so I can snatch pockets of time whenever they present themselves. I still haven't finished it but I can tell you that I LOVE it. I can't believe you wrote it in such a short period of time, it flows so beautifully. You truly have a gift! All my love."

— Jacqueline Rumpel, Miami Beach

Elisabet's transparency in Come Fill the Gap (CFTG) translates into a bold and powerful personal testimony, and for that alone, it is a must read! She uses her life story and the vulnerability of her past trajectories to underscore, what in my personal opinion, the main intention of the Song of Solomon is; that Jesus' perception of us is completely different from our skewed darkened perception of ourselves. He sees us through the eyes of redemption and love, a love so pure, unconditional and holy that it is hard for us to receive it in its magnitude: we limit the fluidity and abundance of His all consuming love because of our issues-just like the Shulamite when she rejects her lover by telling him 'go away to the mountains.'"

Elisabet's attention to scriptural detail gives us greater insight to God's desire in entering with us into a deeper and more fulfilling relationship, emphasizing that our relationship with Him is the foundation to our spiritual, physical, mental and relational well-being. Her ability to capture the Lord's heart and intention in every scripture of the book is heard in her tone, the deconstruction and understanding of the use of symbolism, choice of narratives, language, timing in her integration of biblical correspondences, movies, and books. There were many instances while reading that I thought: 'For such wisdom is too great for man to know alone.' Thus, evidence of the presence of the Holy Spirit's guidance and workings imprinted in every page of this book.

God used CFTG to fan the flame of intimacy He wants so much with me, to draw me in just a little closer so that I can hear His whispers of how much He loves me and that there is no more shame from the past. Elisabet's courageous disclosure of her struggles resonates the true essence in which Jesus wants us to live: in freedom! Her depiction of our Lord's character refreshed my perception of my bridegroom and challenged me to ask, 'Where is it that I am not allowing Him to Come Fill The Gap?' and most importantly, to surrender those skewed perceptions of who our Lord is not : a God who is holding a scoring board next to our name with checks and minuses. Bravo Elisabet! For you have truly communicated God's heart in your in depth research, meditation and relentless search of our Lord's words in Song of Solomon!!"

— Sambra Zaoui, LMSW

"I also enjoyed Elisabet's testimony very much. She has an incredible grasp on the Word, and demonstrates an incredible desire to make much of Christ through her testimony. I so appreciated her authenticity, but not camping on the struggle with sin, but on the incredible grace poured out upon her life."

— Amy Denning, Boston

Come, Fill the Gap

30 DAYS IN THE SONG OF SOLOMON

Elisabet L. Fountain

Come, Fill the Gap

30 Days in the Song of Solomon

Elisabet L. Fountain

Cover: Heather & J. P. Funk
http://heatherfunk.com

Unless otherwise noted, all Scripture quotations are from the New King James Version. Any emphasis is the author's.

ISBN: 0989282805
ISBN 13: 9780989282802

Acknowledgments

All I am is Yours, Jesus, my soul's refuge and delight! I can never thank You enough for finding me, re-creating me, and then pouring your delicious love through me. You are bread for my hunger and wine for my thirst.

My man, your firm and tender oneness with me never ceases to amaze - the cowboy and the gypsy in one. Your affirmation and partnership in this venture give me wings.

Brita, now sweetening the great cloud of witnesses (Hebrews 12:1), you placed my trembling life in His hands and taught me to look into His eyes. You are His most beautiful love letter to me.

David and Serenity, thank you for sharing me so generously with the many people in this, our rich, abundant life. Your understanding exceeds mere acceptance; you are embracing your own callings in releasing me to mine. I adore you!

Vicky Bentley, Lisa Keeler, Steve Cole, and Dr. William Iverson, independently from each other, yours were the voices that repeatedly urged me to write. Thank you for listening to the Holy Spirit, while I was shrugging Him off.

Amy Simonson, my precious support and friend, thank you for enduring dashes and transforming wayward sentences into readable English! Thank you for how you are my friend!

Heather and J.P Funk, what an absolute luxury for me that you interpret the abstractions in my mind into gorgeous visual art!

My beloved Oasis sisters, you are my weekly inspiration! Because of your trust and shoulder-to-shoulder partnership in this great adventure, I press in deeper for His treasures. If you only knew how much this means!

Sira Veciana-Muino, who does what you did, offering legal expertise without being asked! Thank you for your eagerness and tenacity in detangling all the logistics that would otherwise paralyze me. Such a blessing!

To Jacqueline Rumpel, my delightful friend, who tediously corrected the manuscript, thank you is not enough!

McChesney family, how rare and priceless that our very first meeting whispered the promise of our unique partnership in life. And now, visions braided onto one adventure, I can never thank you enough for your love, your trust, and the way you back every word by action. We know this is an honor, and we treasure it zealously!

Foreword

have never read a commentary on this Song Of Songs that shared
as incite-fully the real heart and intent of why it is included in the
cannon of Holy Scripture as what has been written by our dear
sister.

As a pastor and preacher to men I have made much of the creation
of gender by GOD. I do maintain that HE is revealing much to us
about Himself by taking his likeness imparted to Adam and then
dividing that likeness into two very similar, yet very different people
when HE created woman. That there are things we can only know
about our FATHER by seeing it in an earthly mother just as we may
learn much about HIM in seeing a human father is, to me, a wonderful arrangement.

Our GOD also created the circumstances where romance could
bring two back together into oneness that would allow us the
opportunity to know something of the relationship that our Christ
would have with us individually and corporately.

The real purpose of our passions is to draw us to their ultimate fulfillment in the romance of Christ the groom WHO would win us as
HIS bride. Unfortunately, we, as lost descendants of Adam and Eve,
go about gratifying passions in such a way that they not only fail to
fulfill that purpose they become false gods that enslave our hearts.

Elisabet has shared her discoveries in this quest for fulfillment of
passion together with insights into poetic scripture that reveal the
work of the Holy Spirit and the fruit of her husband's ministry to her.

I say to all men who would allow themselves to be blessed to humble themselves and receive that which their sister shares. She "prophesies with her head covered".

I say to my sisters who would be blessed, hear well the lessons this divine romance teaches through their fellow daughter of Eve.

Ken Graves
Pastor
Calvary Chapel, Bangor, ME

TO BRITA

There are people
Who love me and give me the very best they can
And it's not enough.

There are people
Who look to me for love and attention
And I want to be what they need
But I cannot.

There are things to be done,
And I stretch to be a doer,
But they are too big and too many
- I always fall short.

You are limitless love
And Creator of visions
Come fill the gap.

As a dancer's body or a singer's voice
So are we His song to this world

Invitation

*Only he who flings himself upward when the
pull comes to drag him down, can hope to break
the force of temptation. Temptation may be an
invitation to hell, but much more is it an opportunity
to reach heaven. - Charles H. Brent[1]*

I t felt like an appendix ruptured. Only it was my temper oozing sick and yellow over my 13-year old daughter, spewing on her my guilty awareness that I was falling short all over the place.

All she had done was ask me to take her ice skating.

But we were in a season where my ever-busy husband was gone for months, and as a homeschooling mother of two teens, part-time teacher, leader of a thriving ministry, and solely responsible for running the household, (the rehearsed list is always ready on my tongue) - her innocent request was the needle that punctured the swollen, infected appendix of my conscience and frustration.

I can't take you anywhere! Ever!

And then we both cried long enough for the pent-up tension to subside and His comfort to ease its way into our feverish souls. After apologizing and assuring her, alone in my room, I became the daughter receiving my heavenly Father's assurance - but not as I expected.

My life is too big! Make it smaller, so I can manage it.

Now, was that not a reasonable request - just like hers?! He had it in His power to do it for me. Any minute now, He would show me which of my responsibilities were too much - which ones He would discharge. But ever untamable, my Father did not submit to the counsel from the self-help books about balance and me-time. He did not stroke my self-pity and assure me that this indeed was much too much to expect from one woman. In fact, He sounded nothing like my self-soothing thoughts.

Instead, in that way you just know in your DNA it is God speaking to you, He breathed over me. *No, I will make you stronger instead. You asked me to take you the higher way, so I will. You are not enough. I will fill the gap.*

He was referring to countless commitments I had made over the years in worship, in devotion, in awareness of His majesty and incredible goodness. In lucid moments, I had breathed in the stillness of knowing He is God. In moments of intimacy I had whispered, *YES, Your highway of holiness is the only way for me.* I had seen glimpses of higher heights and deeper seas and freely surrendered to His sovereignty in my life. He remembered every word and now reminded me.

And just like that, the Chiropractor adjusted the spine of my world view, and my mind began to align. It changed everything.

There are countless helpful books on how to manage time, better a marriage, raise kids, minister to women — and I have gratefully reaped many practical fruits from them.

However, it's my experience that God is not quite as manageable as I would like, and He doesn't always play by the rules of those books.

In fact, when I journey through the lives described in the Bible, most of them are not convenient like that either.

Though we learn techniques from these how-to books, reality has a way of messing up our systems. This book is for those of us whose lives are too big and whose hearts are too hungry - who cry out, **Come, Fill the Gap.**

WHY SONG OF SOLOMON?

As long as I can remember, I've been aware of my soul's appetite. Even as a little girl I was craving more intimacy, eye contact, intensity than was available, and I didn't know what do with this gnawing longing.

Later, when I discovered Jesus' incredible, redeeming love, I still had the perception that He was so 'proper' that the **real** me was unwelcome. The actual person inside cried out to be seen, to be touched, to live in the affection of a Hollywood movie. I feared I would be too much for Him — would need to be sanitized. Maybe when I became spiritual enough, the cries would go away.

But they didn't. And I fell into sin with a woman who had equally suppressed her desire for beauty and tenderness - qualities both of us thought were only found in another woman's eyes. We saw in each other the echo of our own dream. So deep was the pull because it was mixed with the God-given longing for beauty and eternity. We shared a yearning that was polluted the minute we thought we might fulfill it in each other. Rather than standing shoulder to shoulder with our faces towards Him, we turned towards each other and in that unholy embrace, turned our backs to Him.

"He has made everything beautiful in its time. Also He has put eternity in their hearts, except that no one can find out the work that God does from beginning to end." Ecclesiastes 3:11

We had placed in each other the hope for something God alone can deliver; and no matter the object, women do it all the time.

Having enough sense to break it off, to repent and commit myself to accountability, I found myself at home with my Bible, asking, **What do I do with this ache?**

And as I opened the Song of Solomon, I found on these holy pages a passion, full-blooded, unashamed, and holy. Pure. My Savior's love for me. A love so committed that in its flame, I became pure. And my desire had a legitimate, safe direction where I didn't have to hold back. Not only was I loved in return, I was the one responding, not initiating.

The more I surrendered to this fiery, devoted Lover, the more I became His, the more I became me. It's my life's prayer that I might draw others to the free, fantastic journey into holy love beckoning from the pages of Song of Solomon. **Not a scholar,** I am simply a fellow sojourner, who has discovered a Paradise I just can't keep to myself.

I've been surprised at the warfare that's surrounded this study. Repeatedly, the internet, the computer, and even the power have shut down. I spent the night before first teaching this to my beloved women at Calvary Chapel Miami Beach in the ER unnecessarily.

So I have a hunch that there's more power and freedom here than even I have a clue about, and I pray with my whole being that these verses fall in receptive soil — that we will allow Him to take all of us. With that in mind, I have provided questions for reflection throughout the book. The blank lines are intended for you to capture your own love song, as you respond to His Voice.

A BEAUTIFUL MYSTERY

Many people, especially in modern times, read this passionate litera-
ture merely as a key to human marriage. And there are countless
treasures here for that purpose. On the other hand, I have heard
some skeptics dismiss it because of Solomon's notorious womaniz-
ing. What could a man of more than 1000 lovers, who grew increasingly dissatisfied with life, teach us about God's design for marriage?!

We cannot grasp the relentless redemption of God! Solomon's parents, David and Bathsheba, engaged in a reckless affair that led to
the murder of Bathsheba's husband and the death of their firstborn
son, the fruit of their sin. And God forgave. And He redeemed to
the degree that Solomon (whose name reflects God's quality as
the Prince of Peace) was the one to build the magnificent temple of
God. He was the one so pleasing to God when he asked for wisdom
that God additionally lavished riches and honor on him.

"And God gave Solomon wisdom and exceedingly great understanding, and **largeness of heart** like the sand on the seashore." I Kings 4:29

Yes, Solomon became ensnared by the women and the wealth and
the utter meaninglessness of those pursuits - but assuming that
every Word of the Bible is God-breathed, His Creator redeemed
this Song, like He did Proverbs and Ecclesiastes by this author, to
express to us **His** wisdom, exceedingly great understanding, and
largeness of heart.

The Thompson Chain Reference Study Bible provides this synopsis:
*This book has been severely criticized because of its amorous language.
Its right place in the Bible has been defended by many saintly souls in all
ages. They have regarded it as a spiritual allegory, representing the holy
affections existing between God and His chosen people, or Christ and*

His church. It is an oriental poem, the ardent expression of which can only be properly interpreted by a mature spiritual mind. The Bridegroom represents Christ; the Bride, the church.[2]

For me, the stunning beauty is that the two interpretations intertwine. Over and over throughout the entire Cannon, God refers to Himself **as a Groom with His Bride** or **as a Husband with His wife**. Isaiah 61:10, Isaiah 62:5; Matthew 9:15, Mark 2:19, Luke 5: 34, John 3:29

"FOR THIS REASON A MAN SHALL LEAVE HIS FATHER AND MOTHER AND BE JOINED TO HIS WIFE, AND THE TWO SHALL BECOME ONE FLESH. This is a great mystery, but I speak concerning Christ and the church." Ephesians 5:31-32

It is a great mystery, especially when we consider the New Jerusalem.

"Then I, John, saw the holy city, New Jerusalem, coming down out of heaven from God, prepared as a bride adorned for her husband." Revelation 21:2

In this book we will not dissect the mystery like a butterfly pinned down. We will enjoy the Beauty and the Voice beckoning us into a realm where longings are free and passions run deep.

"And the Spirit and the bride say, **Come**, and let him who hears say, **Come**! And let him who thirsts come. Whoever desires, let him take the water of life freely." Revelation 22:17

Come, desire with me.

Let's drink freely and deeply from the water of life.

DAY 1
Your Love is Better than Wine

*If Christians are forbidden to enjoy the wine of
the Spirit they will turn to the wine of the flesh....
Christ died for our hearts and the Holy Spirit
wants to come and satisfy them. - A.W. Tozer[3]*

1 Kings 13 narrates a story where a man of God was sent to rebuke the king. He had the courage and obedience to confront the king with the Word of the Lord at risk of his own life; but after his mission was done, he was deceived by another man who called himself a prophet. Somehow, he was sufficiently acquainted with His Master's voice well enough to obey, even at great risk - but not well enough to perceive when it was imitated.

Solomon's own life is an illustration of someone who did amazing things for the Lord, but lost his way personally, because he allowed human desires to drown out the Lord's conviction in his life. The wisest man who ever lived, and possibly the richest ever, gave himself over to all the world has to offer - only to find it was meaningless. He became a fool. It was too little - not too much. His soul remained hungry - as when we gorge ourselves on junk food and feel sick, not satisfied.

When Solomon's father David was confronted with the greed behind his demanding another man's wife, God's rebuke was not:

When are you going to be content?! Enough already! Stop wanting so much. The rebuke was not towards the "largeness of heart", I Kings 4:29, which He bestowed as a gift to Solomon. It was that David **took**, rather than allowing God to **give:**

"I gave you your master's house and your master's wives into your keeping, and gave you the house of Israel and Judah. And if that had been too little, I also would have given you much more!" 2 Samuel 12:8

I also would have given you much more. Religion teaches us a restrictive *You're too much! Want less; sin less; be less.* The Biblical Lover of our souls, contrarily, invites us in deeper, higher - much more! Rather than further drying up the places deep within us that are panting for water, as so many of us have misguidedly assumed, He is affectionately devoted to personally touching these raw or hardened places with His revitalizing water and wine. Perhaps, like pets who learned to fear their master's hand, we have inadvertently shied away from Jesus, thinking His hand would be harsh as well. But oh, He is altogether different from anyone we have ever known.

Come closer and let's tune our hearts towards this highest song.

SONG OF SOLOMON 1:2

"Let him kiss me with the kisses of his mouth!
For your love is better than wine."

MAIN CHARACTERS:

- The royal Lover, Solomon, whose name contains Shalom
- The Beloved, the Shulamite, whose name is a female reflection of Solomon
- The daughters of Jerusalem, her friends who are not yet His beloved

LITERARY TREASURES

The implication of **wine**, from a root verb meaning **to effervesce**,[4] is that of banqueting wine. Not mere survival, it is about celebration. Perhaps celebration is essential for soul survival? The word used for **love** has a strong sexual flavor. It is imperative for our unlocking this treasure to put aside any pastel colored, churchy visual. This is red hot. It is where our deepest emotions reside.

Notice the shift from third to second person. *This kind of switch is quite common in Hebrew poetry and is not uncommon in love poetry from other ancient cultures. It is as if she begins by thinking about him and then almost unconsciously she is speaking to him.*[5] Reading the Psalms, we find the same dual awareness, as the Psalmist marvels at God's majesty and then seamlessly turns his attention from the wonders to the heart of God Himself.

COME, FILL THE GAP

The Kisses of His Mouth - Most prostitutes (whose livelihood it is to perform romantic fantasies) draw the line at kissing on the mouth. It's too personal. Time and again their stories align: surviving sexual abuse in childhood, they coped by severing their soul from their body. As trained by their malefactors, the physical shell becomes a stock and supply of silver. Whatever will pay. But no kisses on the mouth – too close to the soul!

A baby's first experience of pleasure is warm milk through tiny lips. An insecure child clings to his pacifier - an insecure adult bites her lip or overeats or smokes or drinks. The mouth is associated with our deepest needs and longings.

Our Lover immediately aims directly at the core of our soul. He is setting a tone of intimacy, of acceptance of the authentic as opposed to the religious, the polished, the tame. The indie Christian band Deas Vail renounced that safe, passionless knock-off copy of His full-blooded romance with us: *I can't believe in this, this blue-lipped life-less kiss*[6]

As C.S. Lewis so famously described it: *Of course He's not tame! But He is good!*[7]

And that makes all the difference!

When I first engaged Christian counseling, 23 years old, newly saved, I had never questioned that I was a lesbian. Reluctantly realizing it to be outside God's will, I still knew no other way to feel alive than to immerse myself in the colorful world of art. Dancing flamenco was already my identity; it was how I expressed the fire inside, and more importantly, how I gained the attention that was my opium. Like any other drug, there was an escalating pull for more, more. And no matter the size of the sea of dance and concerts, no matter whose affirmation I managed to attract, it only deepened my despair for more — thirsty, surrounded by salt water, lost, alone, trapped, dying...

So in counseling, I erupted in frustration: *What kind of cruel joke is this: first He makes me able to see how tender and precious women are - and then He forbids me to love them! He begets me a wildfire and demands I play the candle!*

Brita, my counselor, looked at me with eyes profoundly at rest. I sensed His twinkle in her eyes, as she asked, *Do you really think your passion is greater than His? Do you really think you know better how love thrives?*

Might it be possible that He didn't bend your attractions in this direction, but that He can straighten them? Your river is not too strong; it's just in need of some stronger banks so the water can rush in the right direction without overflowing and causing damage and becoming muddy.

She is in hospice care out of my reach, as I write this, my life-long friend who has mentored me through many a confusing season throughout my life. She has lived so many decades of trusting devotion to the Savior, Redeemer, and as she faces the last minutes of her devouring cancer, I hear her whisper what became her life's song, *I rest in the arms of the One who has never failed me.* She used to sing verses from this highest Song as comfort to me and devotion to Him. I know He is singing over her now.

Better Than Wine - Wine in this culture was purer than water. It was safer to drink. But the implication from the Hebrew context is banqueting wine - celebration. The association is high spirits - the sweetest earthly joys. Your love is **better** than that!

Earthly wine, like earthly love, can be detrimental! Without self-control and surrender to His Spirit, without His love flowing in our veins, the best things may become deadly. A stifling mother's love, obsessive exercise, gluttonous food, codependent friendships, and controlling relationships are just a few examples of a million varieties of earthly wine turning toxic.

That's why His love is **better.** There's no hang-over; there's no regret. Like a sculptor with a chisel, His love chips away at what hides our true selves. He who designed us loves us into the design where we are most alive and He is most glorified.

SEARCH ME, O GOD, AND KNOW MY HEART

- *Is my life more a blue-lipped, lifeless kiss or a kiss from His mouth?*

- *Am I kissing Him back, or am I withholding my affection?*

- *Why?*

- *Are earthly wines intoxicating me?*

- *Lord, Your love is better than…*

DAY 2

Fragrances

You called, You cried, You shattered my deafness,
You sparkled, You blazed, You drove away my
blindness, You shed Your fragrance, and I drew in
my breath, and I pant for You. - Augustine[8]

SONG OF SOLOMON 1:3-4

"Your anointing oils are fragrant; your name is oil poured out; therefore virgins love you. Draw me away! We will run after you. The king has brought me into his chambers. We will be glad and rejoice in you. We will remember your love more than wine. Rightly do they love You."

LITERARY TREASURES

This is the only time the word *name* is mentioned in this Song. Commentaries disagree on the implications of the term **king**, though the royal titles *my king* and *my queen* are commonly used in ancient love poetry. Perhaps that is why *name* is mentioned here, so early in the love story, reminding the beloved believer of our King of Kings' numerous names and thus multifaceted ways of relating to us.

Messiah literally means **the Anointed One**, and oil is consistently associated in Scripture with anointing.

To be 'anointed' is, among other things, to be made sacred (consecrated); to be set apart and dedicated to serve God; to be endowed with enabling gifts and grace; to be divinely designated, inaugurated, or chosen for some purpose. The Bible Dictionary mentions only two types of anointing: with oil or the Holy Ghost. In short, anointing and oil are much more integrally related than most people realize, which explains why Bible translators sometimes use anoint and oil interchangeably as synonymous verbs. (e.g., Isa. 21:5)[9]

The anointing oils directly point to His healing anointing as in Isaiah 61:1 "The Spirit of the Lord GOD is upon Me, because the LORD has anointed Me...The graces that surround His person," Psalm 45:7-8, in its fullest sense, apply to Him. The holy anointing oil of the high priest (which it was death for anyone else to make) implies the exclusive preciousness of Messiah's name. Exodus 30:23[10]

The word translated **draw**[11] is used elsewhere in the Old Testament to describe a powerful attraction of love. The prophet Hosea speaks of God drawing His people to Him with attraction and love. Hosea 11:4[12] This romantic Song is like a concentrated, condensed taste of the entire Divine invitation beckoning from Genesis through Revelation.

COME, FILL THE GAP

Today's Miami Herald ran a story on how hotels in South Beach are deliberately using fragrances to **connect at a deeper level with their customers.** Each hotel blends a signature mix to etch a pleasant association into the guest's subconscious memory. Fragrance raises memories from dark fathoms beneath our logical awareness. It, like the kisses of His mouth, connects with something much deeper, much closer to our core.

"Oil and perfume make the heart glad." Proverbs 27:9

Like the haunting sweetness of a song, fragrances have the power to transport us to realms more akin to dreams and movies than our factual day-to-day existence. No matter when or from whom the scent of my grandfather's cologne drifts my way, it sweeps me back to summer days under colossal shading trees. Instantly, all my senses are awakened to that experience - the roughness of northern strawberries on my tongue and grandmother's off-beat laughter. Somehow these memories feel truer than brick and mortar reality. Perhaps the part of us that travels on these aromas is the truer part, the eternal…

And how we long for it. As when a movie transitions to slow-motion - abridging a life or an experience with a song - isn't there a sense that we should have our own sound track? Why is it such a common fantasy to imagine our own funerals? Could it be that deep down we feel robbed by the lack of emotional intensity and presence, buried under the practical realities that encage the truest part of us.

If only we grasped how fragrant we already are! We do have a sound track; He is singing over us:

"The LORD your God in your midst, The Mighty One, will save; He will rejoice over you with gladness, He will quiet you with His love, He will rejoice over you with singing." Zephaniah 3:17

And like the sophisticated hotels of South Beach, we radiate an unforgettable fragrance:

"Now thanks be to God who always leads us in triumph in Christ, and through us diffuses the fragrance of His knowledge in every place. For we are to God the fragrance of Christ among those who are being saved and among those who are perishing. To the one we are the aroma of death leading to death, and to the other the aroma of life leading to life. And who is sufficient for these things?" 2 Corinthians 2:14-16

We are not sufficient. We are inherently insufficient - Oh, come, fill that gap!

And yet, God is diffusing through us the fragrance of His knowledge in every place. To Him, we are the fragrance of Christ; we carry the scent of His Name poured out. I long to be a stronger, sweeter, freer fragrance; less diluted and disguised by pride and agenda. And I think of the two Mary's who anointed Jesus feet:

"Then Mary took a pound of very costly oil of spikenard, anointed the feet of Jesus, and wiped His feet with her hair. And the house was filled with the fragrance of the oil." John 12:3

His Name is oil poured out; therefore the virgins love Him. And the response of those who love Him is to pour out their costly oil at His feet. Like an elegantly sweeping, waltz, twirling around over the dance floor in a secure embrace, sometimes we see His generosity, sometimes the response of the Bride. There's this ever-flowing give and take expressed in its music; she will give Him the treasure of her heart in prayer, and He will speak those same words back to her laced with His authority and redemption.

His anointing oils are fragrant - and my heart yearns to pour out the costliest oils of my life over His wounded feet. In the process I diffuse in every place the fragrance of His knowledge, while to God I smell like Christ.

"Draw me away! We will run after you. The king has brought me into his chambers. We will be glad and rejoice in you. We will remember your love more than wine. Rightly do they love you." Song of Solomon 1:4

Realizing that this fragrance, this love, is more real than any earthly wine, and that He always leads us in triumph in this dance, draw me away! And immediately, immediately, I am brought into His chamber.

Both Mary of Bethany and Mary Magdalene were scorned for their shameless display of adoration, but Jesus went above defending them:

"Let her alone. Why do you trouble her? She has done a good work for Me. For you have the poor with you always, and whenever you wish you may do them good; but Me you do not have always. She has done what she could. She has come beforehand to anoint My body for burial. Assuredly, I say to you, wherever this gospel is preached in the whole world, what this woman has done will also be told as a memorial to her." Mark 14:6-9

After solemnly warning His disciples about the signs and the tribulations at the end of the age in Matthew 24, He follows up by a curious parable about ten virgins, five of whom had enough oil to wait out the night before the bridegroom appeared, and five of whom did not. Not only were those without oil foolish; they were outside the reach of help from the wise virgins. "Your name is oil poured

out; therefore virgins love you." Song of Solomon 1:3 Like the ador-
ing women anointing his feet for burial, it may be costly for the
wise virgins to keep enough oil for the long night before His return.
But how much more pricey to be found without oil at his return!
Whatever the consequences of wearing His Name now, consider
the alternative....

"Watch therefore, for you know neither the day nor the hour in
which the Son of Man is coming." Matthew 25:13

SEARCH ME, O GOD, AND KNOW MY HEART.

- *Am I more concerned with other's perception
  of my fragrance than with Yours?*

- *Am I free to worship You openly? If
  not, what are my reservations?*

- *How do I best pour out my costly oil?*

- *How can I honor Your Name today?*

- *Oh, Jesus, I may not be like either Mary, but I am me, and I long to worship you more deeply in my life. Take what I am and what I am not - and let it become like perfume from an alabaster jar to You.*

Come, Fill the Gap

DAY 3
Whose Vineyard to Keep?

*The most radical treatment for the fear of man
is the fear of the Lord. God must be bigger to
you than people are.* - Edward T. Welch[13]

SONG OF SOLOMON 1:5-6

*"I am dark, but lovely, O daughters of Jerusalem,
like the tents of Kedar, like the curtains of Solomon.
Do not look upon me, because I am dark, because
the sun has tanned me. My mother's sons were
angry with me; they made me the keeper of the vineyards, but my own vineyard I have not kept."*

LITERARY TREASURES

Some translations employ *black*, rather than *dark*, but the Hebrew word[14] simply indicates someone darkened by the sun. The conjunction *but* links together two different but equal entities. *Dark* and *lovely* are equally strong, equally true.

Daughters of Jerusalem: In a wedding, these are the attending bridesmaids. Jamieson, Fausset, and Brown suggest they are *those invited to Gospel blessings, so near to Jesus Christ as not to be unlikely to find Him*. They are weaving in and out of this Song, and we will consider them in more depth later.

Tents of Kedar were made of the skins of black goats. Kedar was a territory southeast of Damascus where the Bedouin roamed. *The curtains of Solomon* might refer to *the rich tapestries adorning the walls of the royal palace and therefore intended to be a contrast to the dark tents of Kedar, just as the girl's attractiveness is in contrast to her dark skin.*[15]

Notice *my mother's sons* – not *my brothers*. Implying distance, this verse echoes the absolute call to separation unto Him. This is delightfully expressed in Psalm 45:10-11: "Listen, O daughter, Consider and incline your ear; Forget your own people also, and your father's house; So the King will greatly desire your beauty; Because He is your Lord, worship Him."

COME, FILL THE GAP

In this verse, *dark* has nothing to do with race! As we see in verse 6, darkness refers to being tanned by the sun; tainted by this world. We are in this world but not of it, which is quite a balancing act. When Jesus washed the disciples' feet, he made the distinction: "He who is bathed needs only wash His feet, but is completely clean." John 13:10

There's this split consciousness at the same time of our darkness and yet of His love's complete cleansing.

"You are already clean because of the word which I have spoken to you." John 15:3

We are clean and we are dirty. We are lovely and we are aware of our sinfulness. I don't know that we ever get past this schizophrenia this side of Heaven, and perhaps, in a way it's healthy, cultivating a tension of humility and awareness of sin, so He can convict us. If we accept that both are true, so much stress is eased. We're not surprised by the sin within; we don't have to pretend it's not there - we can live authentically in that truth. The more I repose in His unconditional love, the more I perceive my own humanity. I wish to sin less; it is heart-breaking to cause Him pain. But I am not surprised when I do.

"Do not look upon me, because I am dark, because the sun has tanned me. My mother's sons were angry with me; they made me the keeper of the vineyards, but my own vineyard I have not kept." Song of Solomon 1:6

The sun tans us – the world leaves its marks. That's why it is so dangerous to have an external measure of holiness or righteousness. How quickly our well-intended, Christian culture of fine personal convictions becomes an unspoken code of measuring each other's maturity. Human wisdom becomes so ingrained in our thinking that the line between Scripture and culture is obscured.

The Pharisees fused man-made piousness with Scripture, and it became an ungodly, controlling union. Underneath religious correctness, their hearts, like planets distant from the sun, were much further away from His heart than those of the sinners they disdained. We are both dark and lovely, and what matters to Him is that we turn our hearts towards His light, allowing Him to illuminate us, that

He might take us into His chamber, so we abide with Him instead of performing for Him or for the praise of men.

"For they loved the praise of men more than the praise of God." John 12:43

"How can you believe, who receive honor from one another, and do not seek the honor that comes from the only God?" John 5:44

Living for the honor of one another directly competes with seeking the honor of the only God. We see it here in verse 6: "My mother's sons were angry with me; they made me the keeper of the vineyards, but my own vineyard I have not kept." Song of Solomon 1:6

When we begin to bear His fruit, others often want something from us because His fruit attracts. Whether they are well-intentioned or unsure how to invite Him into the gap, their hunger or demand is often directed at us with the ever present tone of **because you are a Christian**.

And I have received my share of disappointed anger from people who felt entitled to my time or affection as their pastor's wife. It is painful and difficult, because everything in me wants to please and appease; we are designed to bear fruit. I relate to the yearning behind the demand and I wish to bring His healing.

> "You did not choose Me, but I chose you and appointed you that you should go and bear fruit, and that your fruit should remain, that whatever you ask the Father in My name He may give you. These things I command you, that you love one another." John 15:16-17

In the entirety of John 15, fruit, joy, and obedience are linked together and this concept is so often what burns out well-intentioned Christians.

Sometimes in aiming for obedience, we transform from branches bearing fruit back into machines of human productivity - more like factories than vineyards. As it did with Martha, this happens when we allow our attention to be consumed with the work in front of us at the expense of our attention at His feet. Like a flower cut from its root, joy cannot survive independently from abiding in Him. When the joy slips away, it's an indicator that something's wrong in the equation.

Listening to women in search of God's heart is one of my chief joys in life. It is an honor when they invite me into their pursuit of His will, and nothing is more rewarding than being part of guiding a trembling, hurting human hand into His safe, firm grasp. So when I find myself dodging deep conversations and fantasizing of building an impenetrable wall around me, it is evidence that something's wrong. My own vineyard is parched.

Unlike Him, I am limited in time and ability. Unlike Him, the time I devote to one person is at another's expense. In my case, I am a wife and mother before I am a minister - and I am a disciple at His feet before I am even available to my family. I cannot give what I do not have.

That's where this prayer is so liberating: Come, fill the Gap. Come, minister to the people I cannot. Be to them what I cannot.

"But my own vineyard I have not kept." Song of Solomon 1:6

We may be called to lay down our comforts and our physical lives — but never our spiritual lives.

> "Abide in Me, and I in you. As the branch cannot bear fruit of itself, unless it abides in the vine, neither can you, unless you abide in Me. I am the vine, you are the branches. He who abides in Me, and I in

him, bears much fruit; for without Me you can do nothing." John 15:4-5

That's how Come Fill the Gap became a lifeline to me this fall. While my pastor-husband was gone, I became both mother and father, and some of his responsibilities at church, and at home, spilled over onto me. Some expected more from me than I could give, or that was how I perceived it. I longed for more strength and encouragement from others than they could or should give. Well-intentioned, we all wanted to be there for each other – but we couldn't fill the gaps. Only He could.

I wrote in my journal: *Loneliness penetrates every part of me - even as I am surrounded by love: family, others hoping for my affection. I cannot give them what they want. And my man can't give me what I want. I so painfully crave presence, affection, attention. I glimpse them, yes! But they are gone before I even tasted they were there. Keep my heart alive. Keep me from hardening. Even worse: self-pity, which deceptively feels like life - like a dog chewing on its own wound. I am bleeding empty affection in all directions - a muddy, sloppy mess I can't back up by time or action...Come, fill all these gaps!*

Just like when flying and the flight attendant reminds you that in case of emergency, always fasten your own air mask before you assist your child. Our own vineyard is not to be neglected.

SEARCH ME, O GOD, AND KNOW MY HEART

• *Am I living more in the awareness of my darkness or my loveliness?*

- *Are there people I am angry with because they won't keep my vineyard?*

- *Are others angry with me because I won't keep theirs?*

- *Is my vineyard thriving?*

- *Lord, You who are the True Vine, please bring the joy of your vineyard to mine. I release*

  _____

  from the hooks of my expectations and surrender those expectations to you. Come, fill my gap!

- *Concerning those who expect from me, I pray You, the true Gardener, show me when to toil in their vineyard and when to withdraw to my own. Fill the gap between us with Your love and sovereignty and set us both free.*

Come, Fill the Gap

DAY 4
The Footsteps of the Flock

"Come to Me, all you who labor and are heavy laden,
and I will give you rest. Take My yoke upon you and
learn from Me, for I am gentle and lowly in heart, and
you will find rest for your souls." Matthew 11:28-29

SONG OF SOLOMON 1:7-9

"Tell me, O you whom I love, where you feed your flock, where you make it rest at noon. For why should I be as one who veils herself by the flocks of your companions? If you do not know, O fairest among women, follow in the footsteps of the flock, and feed your little goats beside the shepherds' tents. I have compared you, my love, to my filly among Pharaoh's chariots."

LITERARY TREASURES

He, whom she addressed as her king, is now her Shepherd. ***Tell me*** sounds the call of ***explain, expose***[16]. There is a tone of humility, of not being ashamed to not already know. The primitive root of the verb translated ***rest*** paints the picture of *a recumbent animal with all four legs folded*[17]. While NKJV renders the Hebrew **veils herself,** KJV chooses **turneth aside** to interpret the original verb which contains both meanings. Veiling herself by the flock of His companions is synonymous with turning aside from Him.

Without rebuking her ignorance, He immediately answers her question. His voice is that of Matthew 12:20, "A bruised reed He will not break," tenderly acknowledging her need. ***Fairest***[18] indicates far more than physical beauty; it contains textures of goodness and well-being. Asking Him is in itself turning our hearts towards Him, and it washes away any shame. Psalm 34:5

Strikingly, the words for ***shepherd*** and ***feed***[19] are formed of the same root word. The verb means both **to graze** and **to associate with**. The shepherds are identified by what they do. Communion is exactly that: feeding on the bread and wine as a deepening of oneness. Perhaps foreign to our culture, food and fellowship were inseparable in the Hebrew lifestyle.

COME, FILL THE GAP

At noon, when the sun is beating down and exhaustion sets in — what do we do? When life is predictable, it is easy to rest in faith, but stability is quickly evaporating from our world. As the Day draws closer, we either learn to bloom in the midday heat, or we shrivel like a plant without a root system. Perhaps that's why labor pains gradually increase — to teach us how to live in labor.

Do we know that He wants us to rest in the midst of the struggle? Or do you, like I, often think you have to prove to Him that you're a fighter? Where does your heart need rest right now?

> "There remains therefore a rest for the people of God. For he who has entered His rest has himself also ceased from his works as God did from His. Let us therefore be diligent to enter that rest, lest anyone fall according to the same example of disobedience. For the word of God is living and powerful, and sharper than any two-edged sword, piercing even to the division of soul and spirit, and of joints and marrow, and is a discerner of the thoughts and intents of the heart." Hebrews 4:9-12

Rest requires diligence! It sounds paradoxical. When I am trying to relax into sleep, diligence seems like a hindrance. But rest in the noon day, rest in the midst of life's heat, is not the same as taking a nap. It's more like throwing everything into the life boat of obedience, trusting it will lead to safe harbor. According to Hebrews 4, it requires the soul-searching, piercing, two-edged sword of His Word to prevent us from falling into disobedience. Disobedience is never restful; no matter its initial appeal, it is, at its core, the antithesis of peace. It is chaos and destruction.

> "Thus says the Lord GOD, the Holy One of Israel: *In returning and rest you shall be saved; in quietness and confidence shall be your strength.* But you would not, and you said, *No, for we will flee on horses* - Therefore you shall flee! And, *We will ride on swift horses* - therefore those who pursue you shall be swift! One thousand shall flee at the threat of one, at the threat of five you shall flee, till you are left as a pole on top of a mountain and as a banner on a hill. Therefore the LORD will wait, that He may be

gracious to you; and therefore He will be exalted, that He may have mercy on you. For the LORD is a God of justice; blessed are all those who wait for Him." Isaiah 30:15-18

"Tell me, O you whom I love, where you feed your flock, where you make it rest at noon. For why should I be as one who veils herself by the flocks of your companions?" Song of Solomon 1:7

If we do not seek Him in the noon heat, we very easily drift to other, lesser, even false, shepherds.

Nature abhors a vacuum, so if we don't invite Him into our gaps, someone or something else is apt to fill them. That's why the blue-lipped, life-less kiss is never enough. Religion and good behavior and all the self-help books in the world cannot bring us sustaining shade in high heat. Only the true Shepherd can.

"If you do not know, O fairest among women, follow in the footsteps of the flock, and feed your little goats beside the shepherds' tents." Song of Solomon 1:8

If you don't know how to find Him, you, His dearly beloved, follow in the footsteps of the flock. Follow those who went before – those whose lives you respect, as they have been tempered by trials and temptations and stood the test of time. For some reason, there is fascination with newness, as if the untested and inexperienced is superior. It seems ever since the serpent's deception that the eternal has been questioned by the temporal. Safety is found in the footsteps of the flock, not in following some flashing new shooting star.

"Because My people have forgotten Me, They have burned incense to worthless idols. And they have caused themselves to stumble in their ways, from the ancient paths, to walk in pathways and not on a highway, Thus says the LORD: Stand in the ways and see, And ask for the old paths, where the good way is, And walk in it; Then you will find rest for your souls." Jeremiah 6:16

"I have compared you, my love, to my filly among Pharaoh's chariots." Song of Solomon 1:9

A certain horse is wild, untamed, running free. Isn't that what we've come to describe as beautiful, admirable? But this horse is unprotected; it is completely subject to the elements without the care of a veterinarian. Its food is haphazard and its lifespan probably short. We behold its wild majesty from a distance, but we cannot get close. This was the horse I aspired to be before I knew His redeeming love. It looks so idyllic in movies, but it was the longing for shelter and tenderness that drew me into His stable.

I envision the filly among Pharaoh's chariots like the horses from the stunning performance troop Cavalia. With airy fluidity, they dance and perform without bit or bridle out of a desire to please, and their trust in their trainers is unquestionable. Pharaoh's filly has been meticulously cared for since conception. It is raised, not with cruelty, but with kindness. Its obedience makes it beautiful. This is the horse I now yearn to become: not needing bit or bridle, but easily and delightfully obeying His slightest whisper. This is meekness. Unbounded strength under control.

Solomon himself was a delicately disciplined horse, entrusted the honor of building the temple for God's Name. But He gradually threw off discipline and became increasingly wild.

SEARCH ME, O GOD, AND KNOW MY HEART.

- *Which horse am I?*

- *Are there potent illusions beckoning me into wild areas?*

- *Am I on the path of the ancient flock that leads to peace, or am I in any way following a false shepherd?*

- *Lord, draw me into the path where beauty and peace co-exist. Free me from any deception as to what is good, true, and beautiful. I want to be an expression of Your free, unbridled beauty!*

- *"If you abide in Me, and My words abide in you, you will ask what you desire, and it shall be done for you. By this My Father is glorified, that you bear much fruit; so you will be My disciples. As the Father loved Me, I also have loved you; abide in My love. John 15:7-9*

DAY 5 : THE FOOTSTEPS OF THE FLOCK

DAY 5
Your Eyes Are Doves

*In The Divine Romance[20], Gene Edwards
describes a scene where the Lord is drinking in
the unique relationship between Adam and Eve.*

They are never distracted from one another, for there is no distraction. In their eyes, nothing else exists! She has no blemish; she has no wrinkle. There is nothing imperfect in all her being. He loves her continually. And with abandoned, innocent, unbridled passion, she loves him in return. She has full confidence in her place beside him. No reassurances need be given that he loves her. She never questions, but totally accepts his love. There's no fear of displeasing him or losing him. She is beautiful, she knows that, yet there is no pride. Rather a deep inward knowing the he is lord of all earth, and she is...his perfect mate...and when that wondrous Day arrives, so shall these things be true...of my Eve.[21]

May we dare return His love with abandoned, innocent, unbridled passion!

SONG OF SOLOMON 1:12-15

"While the king is at his table, my spikenard sends forth its fragrance. A bundle of myrrh is my beloved to me that lies all night between my breasts. My beloved is to me a cluster of henna blooms in the vineyards of En Gedi. Behold, you are fair, my love! Behold, you are fair! You have dove's eyes."

LITERARY TREASURES

Spikenard: In Rome, it was the main ingredient of the perfume *nardinum (O.L. náladam)* derived from the Hebrew נרד שבלת *(shebolet nard, head of nard bunch)* which was part of the *Ketoret* used when referring to the consecrated incense described in the Hebrew Bible. It is also referred to as the *HaKetoret* (the incense). It was offered on the specialized incense altar in the time when the Holy of Holies was located in the First and Second Jerusalem Temples. The *ketoret* was an important component of the Temple service in Jerusalem. *Nard* is mentioned twice in the Song of Solomon 1:12 and 4:13.[22]

A spice used for Egyptian embalming, myrrh was among the gifts presented to Jesus by the wise men. *Myrrh is an Arabic word for bitter, and it is considered a wound healer because of its strong antiseptic and anti-inflammatory properties.*[23]

Henna blooms, or in some translations camphire, are used for decorative coloring in practice, but Strong's dictionary adds that the term is also figurative for redemption price. Thus, verse 13 may read "My beloved is to me a rich redemption price."

Also called **The Dead Sea Oasis**, En Gedi is the largest oasis on the western shore of the Dead Sea. *The area was allotted to the tribe of Judah, and was famous in the time of Solomon. (Joshua 15:62) Today, the Israeli kibbutz of En Gedi sits along the southern bank of the Nahal Arugot.*[24]

Doves' eyes - It fascinates me that His first specific description of her beauty is the doves' eyes. *The doves in this region have large and beautiful eyes*[25]; however, the symbolic beauty, the first quality He praises, is a reflection of the Holy Spirit who, in the form of a dove, announced Jesus' Messianic identity at His baptism. Doves represent innocence, gentleness, and constant love.

COME, FILL THE GAP

This picture alludes to the women anointing Him for burial. He is not standing forth in ministry to them; He is resting in a receiving position. I struggle to fathom that I can minister to Him! How can the Creator of the universe be blessed by me? In the passage by Gene Edwards, I am lifted to glimpse some of this wonder, because it is Love's nature to be ever-giving and receiving. Love flowing in only one direction is heroic and messianic, yes! But the tenderness of our Lover receiving from us seems even purer, as it renders Him vulnerable to be hurt by us. Your nards, your tears, your whispers of trust in a fretful night bless Him like healing ointment on a wounded heart.

The alabaster jar must be broken for the fragrance to pour out. (Luke 7:37, Luke 7:38; John 12:3) There is a necessary breaking of our earthly self-protection if His fragrance is to be poured out upon us. As He is on His couch, not an armed Warrior, but a relaxed Lover, so our laying down of arms before Him is endearing and necessary for us to draw into His rest. In an embrace without barricade of sword or shield, we feel each other's heart beat. In surrender to His goodness, trusting that He is our best interest, we loosen our control-grip and relax on the couch with Him. Exhale in His strong arms.

But never forget that He is King. In our crimped and limping world, sometimes familiarity corrodes into disrespect. I saw it again recently, as it is all too common, in a young, newly engaged woman. The early glue of infatuation's enchantment was just beginning to dry, and in the dawn of a lifetime together, she now teasingly jabbed at him. The arrow wounded. This was new territory to her, so she didn't see it hit its mark. But we did. In human relationships, as in our divine romance, the minute the ease and informality of close camaraderie erodes respect, contamination enters in.

"My beloved is to me a sachet of myrrh that lies between my breasts." Song of Solomon 1:13

Myrrh was a burial spice. **Between my breasts** conveys an intense intimacy. His death on the Cross and His leaving Heaven to seek and rescue helpless souls like mine are ever between my breasts. It is my dearest treasure, and if it loses its place between my breasts, my heart grows cold. Without this awareness of His Cross between my breasts, my perspective quickly regresses into entitlement or worse, self-righteousness, as if I had rescued myself. As if the alabaster jar in itself could give the enchanting fragrance without the oil inside. As if...

The awareness is not there to weigh me down in guilt, as I once in poverty believed. Sensing my reluctance to step into His freedom, Brita once asked me to lift my eyes and look at Jesus on the Cross – to lift my eyes and realize that He was looking straight at me.

No! I can't! I'll see a debt which can never be repaid. I'm already crushed under shame and condemnation - I cannot bear more debt!

She didn't argue or give me theological explanations.

Just look at Him!

And somehow, with the terrified eyes of my knotted-up soul, I looked up at the Cross where His eyes met mine. I found no scolding, no demand. Rather, I encountered the warmest, most unreserved, generous love I have ever seen or dreamt of - poured out like nourishing balm on my scraped, parched, splintered self.

That was the moment I was saved. That was the moment I became alive.

The sachet of myrrh that lies between my breasts has kept me for over two decades.

And He responds, "Behold, you are beautiful, my love; behold, you are beautiful; your eyes are doves." Song of Soloman 1:15

He is intimately acquainted with all your burned places, Song of Solomon 1:5, and He repeats His word *beautiful* over you. These divine lips spoke the universe into existence, and He, who cannot lie, proclaims you beautiful; you, His love. He reads in your eyes the longing to be devoted for life and beyond. He finds in your eyes the reflection of His Holy Spirit who descended like a dove, at His baptism. He knows your need for significance. He makes you significant. Just like a man must leave his parents to cleave to his wife, so He left heaven to cleave to you – to rejoice over you. "For as a young man marries a young woman, so shall your sons marry you, and as the bridegroom rejoices over the bride, so shall your God rejoice over you." Isaiah 62:5

No, His love is not blind. Yes, he sees, with perfect vision, flaws and blemishes that cause you to recoil in shame and self-contempt. But, beautiful one, He sees beyond all that to who you are becoming.

Wholly and entirely, He empathizes with what brought you here; patiently and skillfully, He will love you onward from strength to strength until you are safely Home. "Can a woman forget her nursing child, and not have compassion on the son of her womb? Surely they may forget, yet I will not forget you." Isaiah 49:15

SEARCH ME, O GOD, AND KNOW MY HEART

- *Show me what I expect to see in Your eyes. Show me how You see me.*

- *Am I trying to protect my alabaster jar, in any way not yielding to Your will?*

- *What truly lies between my breasts? What do I genuinely hold dearest?*

- *Enable me to take Your Words of beauty deeper into my soul, Lord. Love me and change me, till you see the Holy Spirit's reflection in my eyes. Make me more than I am - come, fill the gap!*

DAY 6 : YOUR EYES ARE DOVES

DAY 6

The Rose, the Lily, and the Apple Tree

A rose must remain with the sun and the rain or its lovely promise won't come true. - Ray Evans[26]

SONG OF SOLOMON 2:1-3

"I am the rose of Sharon, and the lily of the valleys. Like a lily among thorns, so is my love among the daughters. Like an apple tree among the trees of the woods, so is my beloved among the sons. I sat down in his shade with great delight, and his fruit was sweet to my taste."

LITERARY TREASURES

So universal in its symbolism is the rose (Song of Solomon 2:1) that it barely occasions explanation. There are over 100 different species of roses, both cultivated and wild. They grow in a rainbow of colors and vary in size, from as small as 1/2 inch across to a diameter of almost 7 inches. The variety itself speaks volumes of our Creator's delight in diversity. The combination of velvety petals with sharp thorns certainly provokes the wealth of symbolism attached to it. *Mediaeval Christians identified the five petals of the rose with the five wounds of Christ...The red rose was eventually adopted as a symbol of the blood of the Christian martyrs.*[27]

Sharon (Song of Solomon 2:1) is in North Palestine between Mount Tabor and Lake Tiberius. *There is here a tacit reference to its meaning of lowliness. Beauty, delicacy, and lowliness, are to be in her, as they were in Him.*[28] *Valleys* reinforces the picture of humility and depth.

Unlike the rose, the lily (Song of Solomon 2:2) has no thorns. All soft, *Lilies of the Valley* have clusters of small, white, bell-shaped flowers that hang from a strong reedy stalk. There may be a dozen or more blossoms per plant. Their outstanding feature is a sweet fragrance. The scent has even inspired perfumes.[29]

Most trees in a forest are not fruit bearing:

> *Christ may be compared to an apple tree, which is very fruitful; and, when full of fruit, very beautiful; and whose fruit is very cooling, comforting, and refreshing. Christ is full of the fruits and blessings of grace, which are to be reached by the hand of faith, and enjoyed; and as he is full of grace and truth, he looks very beautiful and glorious in the eye of faith; and which blessings of grace from him, being applied to a poor, sensible sinner, inflamed by the fiery law, and filled with wrath and terror, sweetly cool, refresh, and comfort him. The apple tree has been accounted an hieroglyphic of love, under*

> which lovers used to meet, and sit under its delightful
> shade, and entertain each other with its fruit; to which
> the allusion may be.[30]

The word translated **wood**[31] (Song of Solomon 2:3) conveys a crowded experience, a thicket, and **shade**[32] includes the quality of defense. Jesus is that defense in a crowd, the shade on a hot day; He is delight in the midst of pressure.

COME, FILL THE GAP

"Take My yoke upon you and learn from Me, for I am gentle and lowly in heart, and you will find rest for your souls." Matthew 11:29

I am a rose or a lily of the valley. Though different and unique, His yoke fits me perfectly and I find rest for my soul. When worldly ambitions and striving for position or acceptance or validation cease, and I root into the depths of His gentleness, I blossom. When I accept His seasons in my life, even the bitter snows of barren seasons, and trust that His seed in me will bear His fruit, I find rest for my soul.

He is right here, affirming: "As a lily among brambles, so is my love among the young women." Song of Solomon 2:2

The word **brambles** (in other translations thistles or thorns) comes from a root verb meaning **to pierce**. When the soil in the Garden of Eden was cursed, thorns and thistles were among the consequences. (Genesis 3:18) Instead of the designed delight in tending the earth, our work and our lives became excruciating, stress-filled toil. As we died spiritually, we were reduced to mere biological creatures who would return to dust after years of labor. (Genesis 3:19) *Vanity of vanities*, says the Preacher; *Vanity of vanities, all is vanity. What profit has a man from all his labor in which he toils under the sun? All things are full of labor; man cannot express it. The eye is not satisfied with seeing, nor the ear filled with hearing.* Ecclesiastes 1:2,3,18

Into this meaningless existence where nothing truly satisfies, ashes to ashes, dust to dust, our Lover entered. When our Messiah reversed the curse and called us again to walk with Him in the easy freedom of Eve before the Fall, thorns pierced His brow. God's rejection of Him, as He bore our curse, pierced His heart, before the Roman spear.

"As a lily among brambles, so is my love among the young women" Song of Solomon 2:2

As opposed to a rose, a lily forsakes all defense; a lily is a dove, white and harmless. He sees us as lilies among those who pierce, and He sends us as sheep among wolves.

He knows your neighborhood, and He is promising to protect you.

Coming from my somewhat feminist background in Denmark, a man's protection was something I almost thought belittling. I can take care of myself! It was deeply ingrained that I would be thought of as weak (and therefore rejected) should I need or receive a man's protection. Not only did it all turn out to be untrue, it turned out to be unwanted.

Even recently, when my Harley-riding man offered his only helmet, my initial response was, ***Your head is as fragile as mine! Why don't you wear it, and then I avoid getting hat-hair!*** My wonderfully southern gentleman couldn't do it. Every fiber in his masculine soul knew it was wrong. It was against nature and design for him to be protected when his stubborn wife was not, so he couldn't wear it either. In the end, I recognized that I was wrestling against God's design, so I wore the helmet. But more importantly, I yielded to my Father's protection through it. No, He did not fix my hat hair. In fact, it was bad enough that I felt the need to explain it multiple times, and by the end of the night, I wore it as a badge of compliance with God's design.

My Robert was expressing the heart of my Bridegroom, and I am still learning to relax in that goodness.

"As an apple tree among the trees of the forest, so is my beloved among the young men. With great delight I sat in his shadow, and his fruit was sweet to my taste." Song of Solomon 2:3

One of many parallels: as she is among the thorns, so He is among the young men. He is one of many crowding in on you, vying for your heart, but He is the only fruit tree among the fruitless wild trees. His fruit is healing, His roots are in the River of Life, and He invites you to come eat freely and rest in His shade.

You *will* be hungry and tired. If you don't eat His fruit, you'll become so famished that, like the prodigal son, you'll find yourself in a swine pit, hoping for a morsel of swine food.

"A satisfied soul loathes the honeycomb, but to a hungry soul every bitter thing is sweet." Proverbs 27:7

If you feast on His fruit, you'll draw others into life-giving delicacy.

"With great delight I sat in His shadow." Song of Solomon 2:3 When I lived in wind-swept Denmark, I never could understand the value of shade. Who wouldn't prefer the sun?! But now, in hot, humid, tropical Miami, the refreshment found in the shade is explicit. Even the sturdiest beach boy dehydrates and depletes under the beating of the sun.

"The LORD is your keeper; the LORD is your shade at your right hand." Psalm 121:5

"For You have been a strength to the poor, a strength to the needy in his distress, a refuge from the storm, a shade from the heat; for the blast of the terrible ones is as a storm against the wall." Isaiah 25:4

SEARCH ME, O GOD, AND KNOW MY HEART.

- *As the Rose of Sharon and the Lily of the valley, am I content where You plant me?*

- *As I live among thorns, are there words or habits of mine that pierce?*

- *Am I resisting or embracing Your protection?*

- *Lord, You say to take Your yoke upon me and learn from Your lowliness and gentleness; show me in my world what that means. Woo me into Your shade when I am distracted and frantic, and remind me to feast on Your fruit, before I am tempted by the feed in the trough.*

DAY 7
Under His Banner of Love

"And Moses built an altar and called its name,
The-LORD-Is-My-Banner." Exodus 17:15

SONG OF SOLOMON 2:4-7

"He brought me to the banqueting house, and his banner over me was love. Sustain me with raisins; refresh me with apples, for I am sick with love. His left hand is under my head, and his right hand embraces me! I adjure you, O daughters of Jerusalem, by the gazelles or the does of the field, that you not stir up or awaken love until it pleases."

LITERARY TREASURES

Notice His initiative. As she is receiving His continual, committed actions of love, she surrenders to His strength.

The **banqueting house**, where Solomon stored his treasure and the queen of Sheba, were given **all her desires** (1Kings10:13), are by several commentaries considered a foreshadowing of the heavenly feast to come. (Isaiah 25:6 and Revelation 19:8-9)

In war, waving banners signal, not who the warriors are, but for whom they fight and to whom they pledge allegiance. **His love conquered us to Himself; this banner rallies round us the forces of Omnipotence, as our protection; it marks to what country we belong, heaven, the abode of love, and in what we most glory, the cross of Jesus Christ, through which we triumph.**[33](See Romans 8:37; 1 Corinthians 15:57; Revelations 3:21)

Sick with love is an expression of the highest degree of pleasure. God designed our body, soul, and spirit to all have the capacity for ecstasy, I believe, as a foretaste of His complete love, which we cannot yet fully bear. **Israel tasted it when the Lord's glory filled the tabernacle, and afterwards the temple, so that the priests could not stand to minister: so in the Christian Church on Pentecost.**[34]

COME, FILL THE GAP

They are abundantly satisfied with the fullness of Your house, and You give them drink from the river of Your pleasures. Psalm 36:8

The effective evangelist is satisfied with His fruit and enjoying His sweet taste in the calm of His shelter. It's so different to encounter someone who 'has an agenda to get us converted' from someone simply enjoying their Lover.

That is why this Song is so powerful: it saturates the soul and spirit in a most unearthly way. The enemy impersonates and caricatures; but it's a shabby imitation, and the seeking soul discerns the difference.

Under which banner do we march, if not His banner of love? Is it the banner of performance? Or is it the banner of earning love or significance? Perhaps that explains the lust of the reality show; the grasp for 5 minutes of fame is a feverish reach for significance. It seems that having been on TV gives a sense of having come alive, as if the cameras give life. It is easy to ridicule, but I ache at the empty reality behind reality TV. The culture is attempting to slake its thirst in saltwater - to die by its own hand.

To feast under His banner of love may almost appear selfish in that perspective. But remember the instruction of the flight attendant: first affix your own air mask and then help someone else. God sometimes uses jealousy to draw hungry hearts to Himself; we are a living illustration of what He offers freely.

My favorite commentary refers to the banqueting house as the *house of wine* and the raisins, the dried grapes, as **the new wine of the kingdom, the Spirit of Christ Jesus.**[35] The apples are from her apple tree, so her lovesick cry is for more of His Spirit and more of His fruit. There are times in worship when the beauty is almost too much to bear. There are intimate moments where we almost touch a nerve of eternal bliss - and then it's gone. These are tiny appetizers of the real Banquet to come where time and personal limitations no longer quench the bliss.

In most cases this intensity of joy is reserved for the heavenly banquet. Every earthly joy is brief — even the best we can imagine — that's why it's so absolutely foolish to sacrifice the eternal, incredible bliss we crave for something so fleeting!

"His left hand is under my head, and his right hand embraces me!" Song of Solomon 2:6

Place your left hand and your right hand in this embrace and envisage the tenderness - close, face-to-face, protective. This Lover is not beset by attachment disorder; He is completely at ease with intimacy, because He is holy and unpolluted - and it cost Him dearly to be able to hold you like this.

None can pluck from that embrace, John 10:28-30, *His hand keeps us from falling,* Matthew 14:30-31, *to it we may commit ourselves,* Psalm 31:5.[36]

Trust this embrace. Commit your life to this embrace. But remember, it is a commitment. Unlike the Geico commercial where three try to tango, there is only room for two in this dance. Do not flippantly stir up a love like that, until you are ready for it.

Jesus Himself urged us to consider the cost; any love, any choice carries a price. Like the shrewd steward, consider the options carefully and make an informed choice.

"I adjure you, O daughters of Jerusalem, by the gazelles or the does of the field, that you not stir up or awaken love until it pleases." Song of Solomon 2:7

This admonition is repeated in Song of Solomon 3:5 and 8:4, each time when she is the most intimate with Him.

Pay attention to the pleading, the solemn charge from one who has discovered the true. The gazelles and the does of the field are beautiful and free, as is His desire for us. Impatience and lack of self-discipline threaten what we are designed to mature into.

The books or the music in which we thought the beauty was located will betray us if we trust to them; it was not in them, it only came through them, and what came through them was longing. These things— the beauty, the memory of our own past—are good images of what we really desire; but if they are mistaken for the thing itself they turn into dumb idols, breaking the hearts of their worshippers. For they are not the thing itself; they are only the scent of a flower we have not found, the echo of a tune we have not heard, news from a country we have never yet visited."[37]

Heed the continual plea of this book: do not try to awaken love until it pleases. Do not try prematurely to grasp that for which you long:
- Human love: wait for Him to bring it
- Sexual love: keep it within its boundaries
- Any other desire: wait! Let Him bring it to you!

"Show me Your ways, O LORD; Teach me Your paths. Lead me in Your truth and teach me, for You are the God of my salvation; on You I wait all the day. Keep my soul, and deliver me; let me not be ashamed, for I put my trust in You…Let integrity and uprightness preserve me, for I wait for You. (Psalm 25:4-5, 20-21)

He is coming soon! It is worth the wait!

SEARCH ME, O GOD, AND KNOW MY HEART

- *Am I living under Your banner of love
  or have I raised another?*

- *Am I trying to bring someone or something
  into Your embrace that doesn't belong?*

- *Am I as committed as You'd like, or
  am I hesitant to be fully Yours?*

- *Oh, let me so live under Your banner of Love that my
  friends are drawn to your banqueting house! Sustain
  me, Holy Spirit, and feed me those fruits from the River
  of Life, so I, too, can bring your healing to the nations.*

DAY 8

Arise, My Love

Thus, as the shell of a seed, a nut or an egg must be broke before its inner life comes forth, so it is with us: the 'shell' of our outer nature must also break in order to free the Spirit of Christ to arise in our hearts. - Francis Frangipane[38]

SONG OF SOLOMON 2:8-13

"The voice of my beloved! Behold, he comes, leaping over the mountains, bounding over the hills. My beloved is like a gazelle or a young stag. Behold, there he stands behind our wall, gazing through the windows, looking through the lattice My beloved speaks and says to me: 'Arise, my love, my beautiful one, and come away, for behold, the winter is past; the rain is over and gone. The flowers appear on the earth, the time of singing has come, and the voice of the turtle-dove is heard in our land. The fig tree ripens its figs, and the vines are in blossom; they give forth fragrance. Arise, my love, my beautiful one, and come away.'"

LITERARY TREASURES

Voice - the root word implies *To call aloud...proclaim...sing...spark...thundering voice.*[39] *Leaping*: *To let down a bucket (for drawing out water); figuratively, to deliver...lift up.* The Beloved, the Living Word, is bursting with majestic attributes. From these two words alone, we see the entire Gospel: He has called out and proclaimed that He has come to deliver us, to lift us up.

Arise: contains *abide... confirm...endure... strengthen*[40] and thus echoes Christ's repeated **Abide** from John 15. **Winter** is from a root word meaning **to hide**. Thus, because He is lifting us up, our time of hiding is over, and we can arise, abide, and endure.

Fig tree: Matthew 21:19 and 24:32 record Jesus using the fig tree as an indicator of seasons. The first Scripture finds Him cursing a fig tree for not bearing fruit, and the second using it in a parable to help the disciples grasp the signs of the end times. In this love song, He mentions the ripening fig tree along with the blossoming vines (again, sweet tones from John 15) between two *arises*. There is the urging to recognize the season, she is in, to not let it pass her by remaining in hiding.

COME, FILL THE GAP

Inhale and be ravished by His virile, joyful strength. He leaps, as the father to the prodigal son, leaving costumes of propriety behind, because a suffering love was beating in his chest.

He reminds me of David dancing with all His might before the Lord, and disdained by his own wife responds, "And I will be even more undignified than this, and will be humble in my own sight." 2 Samuel 6:22

Jesus is dignity. He defines dignity. But human traditions didn't seem to mean much to him; in fact, He sometimes seemed to consider them hindrances to things of real importance.

"He answered and said to them, 'Why do you also transgress the commandment of God because of your tradition?'" Matthew 15:3

He is leaping over the mountains; bounding over the hills. He is arrested by no obstacle; the baggage that is crushing us, He vaults over, and calls us to come out from under the weight.

He waits behind a wall; a wall I have constructed. So often, the mountains in my life, like stress of financial pressure, quietly build a wall of skepticism or cynicism. In creeps the fear that He will fail me this time, or that He will let me fail because of my own inadequacies, and up goes a self-protective wall, as if I ever could protect myself - as if there was any other goodness than His. He gazes through the window, looking through the lattice.

Oh, how I adore His lack of convention! He is not ashamed to be seen leaping over mountains or gazing through windows. He is not ashamed! He is persistent in pursuit; He wants to be the One to make the wall fall.

"gazing through the windows, looking through the lattice." Song of Solomon 2:9

"Behold, I stand at the door and knock. If anyone hears My voice and opens the door, I will come in to him and dine with him, and he with Me." Revelation 3:20

He never forces – He only invites. But listen to the invitation:

"My beloved speaks and says to me: 'Arise, my love, my beautiful one, and come away, for behold, the winter is past; the rain is over and gone. The flowers appear on the earth, the time of singing has come, and the voice of the turtledove is heard in our land. The fig tree ripens its figs, and the vines are in blossom; they give forth fragrance. Arise, my love, my beautiful one, and come away.'" Song of Solomon 2:10-13

Arise! Tear down the wall, forsake the shame. It is a new season! Don't be manacled to who you used to be; you are now His love, His beautiful one.

Whatever your winter may be, consider this verse. Whatever may have frozen your freedom and assurance, hearken to this verse. Listen until His voice resounds and resonates in your spirit. Arise.

"The time of singing has come." Song of Solomon 2:12 If He has ever given you a new song – if you have ever known His grace – SING. It is warfare and worship and truth! It is warfare, because the soul's enemy flees from such praise. It is worship, as an offer of emotion and experience to Him. It is truth, when the facts of your life are absorbed in His overriding sovereignty. Can you hear Him calling?

"Voice of the turtledove is heard in our land" Song of Solomon 2:12 He calls you His dove! He is the other turtledove. Your voice is heard! Through sleepless nights of unnamed fears, He heeds the cry for understanding and help. The days when hormones and stresses growl through your lips, He alone detects your trapped, authentic voice. Do not allow the world or your mood to cloak His faithfulness!

As turtledoves mate for life, so His devotion surrounds and sustains you through the worst days and the longest nights. In this genera-tion of multiple marriages and divorces, it might seem outside our scope of understanding that some love is indeed unshakable. There is a love that does not look for the escape hatch when things get ugly – even when the ugliness is within us. When grief or shock so dissolve our coherency that regaining a foothold again takes longer than most friends endure, His persistence never wavers.

A human, committed friend may stay with us through gloomy shad-ows - may even listen, encourage, and do everything in their power to help. If you have the gift of such a friend, stop and give thanks. But even they cannot put humpty dumpty together again. They cannot restore shattered nerves or breathe sanity to a crushed mind. Only He can fill those gaps.

"He sets on high those who are lowly, and those who mourn are lifted to safety." Job 5:11 "For thus says the High and Lofty One Who inhabits eternity, whose name is Holy: 'I dwell in the high and holy place, with him who has a contrite and humble spirit, to revive the spirit of the humble, and to revive the heart of the contrite ones.'" Isaiah 57:15

"O my dove, in the clefts of the rock, in the crannies of the cliff, let me see your face, let me hear your voice, for your voice is sweet, and your face is lovely." Song of Solomon 2:14

Take this in. You are protected inside the cleft of Him! He is your rock! You are safe! Do what you are created to do! Respond! Lift your voice. I cannot sing your song, no one but you can. My friend Amy's song is creating the soothing ambiances of the seasons in her home. My friend Nicole's is nurturing children in an orphanage. Eric Liddell's was running. What is yours? Do what you are created to do! Your voice is sweet!

"They looked to Him and were radiant, and their faces were not ashamed." Psalm 34:5

NOT ashamed! Before sin crippled them, Adam and Eve were unashamed in their nakedness. Nothing was hidden or questioned in their free trust in Him, whose entire creation testified that He is good. He has never changed. Our innocence was stolen and our trust destroyed, but He has never changed. The charge against Him was a lie.

What might be stealing your song and hiding your face in shame or condemnation or even accusation that He's not faithful?

SEARCH ME, O GOD, AND KNOW MY HEART

- *How can I be free to leap with You?*

- *Have I built walls between us?*

- *Tell me about my song.*

- *Speak to me, my Beloved, until there are no walls between us and I am free to lift my song to You. I long to hear those Words again and again. Help my soul absorb them and become them. I am Yours.*

Come, Fill the Gap

64

DAY 9

Separation

"For what is highly esteemed among men is an abomination in the sight of God." Luke 16:15

SONG OF SOLOMON 2:15-17

"Catch the foxes for us, the little foxes that spoil the vineyards, for our vineyards are in blossom. My beloved is mine, and I am his. He feeds his flock among the lilies. Until the day breaks and the shadows flee away, Turn, my beloved, and be like a gazelle or a young stag upon the mountains of Bether."

LITERARY TREASURES

Foxes is a generic term, including jackals. They are unremarkable pests; but undetected, they are capable of much harm. Eating only grapes, not the vine flowers, they must be driven out before the grape is ripe.

Until the day *breaks* literally means *breathes*. When Jesus breathes on us, the shadows flee away, as when the disciples assembled in fear and "He breathed on them, and said to them, 'Receive the Holy Spirit.'" John 20:22

The shadows of the Jewish dispensation were dispelled by the dawning of the gospel day. And a day of comfort will come after a night of desertion.[41]

The *mountains of Bether* are a literal place *separated from the rest of Israel by the Jordan* (2 Samuel 2:29), *not far from Bethabara, where John baptized and Jesus was first manifested.*[42] The Hebrew word carries the both the meaning of *cleft*[43] and of *piece of an animal cut in half for a sacrifice.*[44] Some commentaries refer to these mountains as *the mountains of separation*. Thus, this Living Word in one breath refers both to our cleft of separating sin and to the sacrifice needed to atone, to bridge the gap.

COME, FILL THE GAP

In my life, the foxes have been subtle attitude shifts, such as allowing a hint of self-righteousness in relationship with my husband or permitting myself to lash out at the kids. They tell me I'm justified. They cuddle me and assure me that no one understands. They spoil my blossoming vineyard.

They quietly dethrone God in my heart and replace Him with my desires and opinions. My thoughts begin to center around my own agendas, and I lose His fragrance in the process. Oh, that we would know how dangerous these foxes are in their moderation. Their crafty voices echo the Deceiver in the Garden of Eden, as they slip into our vineyards with slick suggestions of rights and things deserved.

> To follow the path of my selfish desire
> Would not be a crime they could see
> I could still play the game – be one to admire
> Pretend things were as they should be.
>
> The thought is as sweet as the serpent's kiss
> Poisoned in its defrauding
> There is not a temptation greater than this:
> To sin while the world is applauding.
>
> Your truth is fighting its way through my flesh
> Finally reaching my soul.
> From the depths of my spirit I sense You bless
> My will, as I give up control.
>
> So often I search for the end
> Of your Grace, but it is in vain
> Despite who I am, Your love makes amend
> Despite what I do, you remain.

"Therefore lift your drooping hands and strengthen your weak knees, and make straight paths for your feet, so that what is lame may not be put out of joint but rather be healed. Strive for peace with everyone, and for the holiness without which no one will see the Lord. See to it that no one fails to obtain the grace of God; that no root of bitterness springs up and causes trouble, and by it many become defiled." Hebrews 12:12-15

"My beloved is mine, and I am his; he grazes among the lilies." Song of Solomon 2:16

He is right here with me, urging me to catch those foxes, to stand up in the dignity He has given me.

But sometimes I welcome them. Sometimes I don't want to make my paths straight. In the very next verse, while calling Him her Beloved, she sends Him away.

"Until the day breaks and the shadows flee away, turn, my Beloved, and be like a gazelle or a young stag upon the mountains of Bether." Song of Solomon 2:17 So in the night, in the shadows with sweet voice, she is revealing, *I want to sin for a while here in the dark. I know you can leap over mountains, so right now, leap over the mountains of separation. Give me some space.*

In a heart-wrenching scene in The Divine Romance, Gene Edwards writes,

> *Out of Egypt had come this girl. She crossed a searing wilderness, and in the land of promise, she found rest and prosperity. But in her prosperity, she moved farther and farther from her Lord...Unnoticed by her, but well observed by her enemies, her wayward wandering from her God had caused her to lose the great strength he had bestowed upon her.*[45]

Ezekiel echoes the same warning:
> "And when I passed by you and saw you struggling in your own blood, I said to you in your blood, 'Live!' Yes, I said to you in your blood, 'Live!' I made you thrive like a plant in the field; and you grew, matured, and became very beautiful. Your breasts were formed, your hair grew, but you were naked and bare. When I passed by you again and looked upon you, indeed your time was the time of love; so I spread My wing over you and covered your nakedness. Yes, I swore an oath to you and entered into a covenant with you, and you became Mine," says the Lord GOD. "Then I washed

you in water; yes, I thoroughly washed off your blood, and I anointed you with oil. I clothed you in embroidered cloth and gave you sandals of badger skin; I clothed you with fine linen and covered you with silk. I adorned you with ornaments, put bracelets on your wrists, and a chain on your neck. And I put a jewel in your nose, earrings in your ears, and a beautiful crown on your head. Thus you were adorned with gold and silver, and your clothing was of fine linen, silk, and embroidered cloth. You ate pastry of fine flour, honey, and oil. You were exceedingly beautiful, and succeeded to royalty. Your fame went out among the nations because of your beauty, for it was perfect through My splendor which I had bestowed on you," says the Lord GOD. "But you trusted in your own beauty, played the harlot because of your fame, and poured out your harlotry on everyone passing by who would have it. You took some of your garments and adorned multicolored high places for yourself, and played the harlot on them. Such things should not happen, nor be. You have also taken your beautiful jewelry from My gold and My silver, which I had given you, and made for yourself male images and played the harlot with them." Ezekiel 16:6-17

The language here is almost crude! This is the Holy Book! I am shocked by how directly God sees and addresses our most passionate and our most private behavior. The mountains of separation follow the little foxes. It's been said,

Sow a thought, reap an attitude
Sow an attitude, reap an action
Sow and action, reap a lifestyle

SEARCH ME, O GOD, AND KNOW MY HEART.

- *Which foxes are in my vineyard?*

- *Which mountains of separation are tempting me?*

- *What do I do about it?*

- *My Beloved, Israel was not immune, and neither am I. If I am in any way using the beauty you've bestowed upon me inappropriately, convict me deeply so that I'm finished toying with foxes.*

- *"Not until we take God seriously will we ever take sin seriously." - R.C. Sproul[46]*

DAY 10
Watchmen

Life is far too difficult and we are far too sinful to live in solitude. We need community. We need accountability. And God has anticipated our need by giving us the local church as the primary means of this accountability. - Tim Challies[47]

Ever the gentleman, He respected her wishes and left her alone as requested. Now she senses the consequence – that her bed is empty; all His comfort and assurances are gone.

SONG OF SONGS 3:1-4

"By night on my bed I sought the one I love; I sought him, but I did not find him. "I will rise now," I said, "And go about the city; in the streets and in the squares I will seek the one I love." I sought him, but I did not find him. The watchmen who go about the city found me; I said, "Have you seen the one I

love?" Scarcely had I passed by them, when I found the one I love. I held him and would not let him go, until I had brought him to the house of my mother, and into the chamber of her who conceived me."

LITERARY TREASURES

The Hebrew *laiyl* translated *night* means *a twist (away from the light)*.[48] The word translated **sought** means **to search out (by any method, specifically in worship or prayer); by implication, to strive after; - ask, beseech, desire, inquire.**"[49] Sometimes it requires the absence of light to arouse in us the energy for this kind of search.

The three *rise now* and *go about* root words all imply resolve - a triple resolve. From **rise** we additionally hear the nuances of **abide ...be clearer, confirm, continue**"[50], and from **now** we hear **entreaty or exhortation**.

Derived from a primitive root meaning **to hedge around (as with thorns)**, **watchmen** contains a multitude of expressions for protection, including **be circumspect...keep...preserve**.[51]

The mention of the mother excludes impropriety, and imparts the idea of heavenly love, pure as a sister's, while ardent as a bride's; hence the frequent title, 'my sister - spouse.' Our mother after the Spirit, is the Church, the new Jerusalem (John 3:5-8; Galatians 4:19, 26); for her we ought to pray continually, Ephesians 3:14-19.

COME, FILL THE GAP

"I sought him, but I did not find him." Song of Solomon 3:2

He will not co-exist with our sin. Never mistake His generous love and boundless assurances for weakness. His grace and forgiveness are not cheap enablers to cover over an unrepentant heart. All the wondrous qualities of His character are holy. His love is holy. His Word is holy. We can gratefully receive their life-giving redemption, but we cannot play games with Him.

"Behold, the LORD's hand is not shortened, That it cannot save; Nor His ear heavy, That it cannot hear. But your iniquities have separated you from your God; And your sins have hidden His face from you, So that He will not hear." Isaiah 59:1-2

In my early years with Brita, while dancing flamenco and in every way exuding the artist persona, I felt like a zombie, neither dead nor alive, during worship in church. I watched others give themselves over into His arms and I tried to copy their moves, hoping likewise to be enraptured. Nothing. There was something blocking my devotion, and I didn't know what to do about it.

How priceless is a praying friend! As Brita prayed for insight, He showed me that my life was so full of my own choices that there was very little space left for him. Like a child's hand clutching its childish treasures, He gently asked if I was willing to release my grip and let those treasures go. My dance, my friends, my identity, even my cat! Was I willing to trust Him with the emptiness they would leave behind?

I think so…

What was the alternative? To remain a zombie - neither sinner nor saint? I couldn't go back to my worldly treasures; I had already looked into His eyes and seen that life-full love. But I couldn't move forward either, watching others worship while I remained behind a glass wall. To join into their worship – to discover my own – my hand had to be emptied to make room for Him.

If it were not for His enabling strength, I could never have done it! The artists I admired most in this world thought I had become brain-washed, and I could see them looking at me thinking, **So sad!** I had to pull away from them. That night I cried on my bed and sacrificed my Isaac, my dance, that which had brought me the deepest illusion of life and worth. That night He called me to leave my country and follow Him into full-time ministry. We made a deal: I would throw overboard all the ropes that fettered me to my old self if He would promise me that I would be allowed to express the passion, the beauty, and the freedom I had loved in flamenco some other way. **Make me an ambassador of Your passion, beauty, and freedom.** Since then, through every season of my life, that has been my pursuit. It has been the paradisial filter though which I've seen the mundane.

When your bed is empty; when you seek the One you love but cannot seem to find Him, ask why. Sometimes it is outright sin – if so, He will convict. Sometimes it's priorities – he will adjust. Sometimes it's exhaustion – he will invite us to rest in his shade. Sometimes, it's just a longing He uses to beckon us in closer.

After Adam and Eve's devastating fall, just like our Shulamite, they wanted distance from God. So they hid themselves from His presence among the trees of the Garden of Eden. Obviously, we can never hide from His presence, but He will respect our boundaries, even as He pleads and reasons with us. In the garden, He respected their shameful hiding; He even covered their nakedness, just like in Ezekiel, and He then asked three questions.

> "And they heard the sound of the LORD God
> walking in the garden in the cool of the day, and

Adam and his wife hid themselves from the presence of the LORD God among the trees of the garden. Then the LORD God called to Adam and said to him, "Where are you?" So he said, "I heard Your voice in the garden, and I was afraid because I was naked; and I hid myself." And He said, "Who told you that you were naked? Have you eaten from the tree of which I commanded you that you should not eat?" Then the man said, "The woman whom You gave to be with me, she gave me of the tree, and I ate." And the LORD God said to the woman, "What is this you have done?" The woman said, "The serpent deceived me, and I ate." Genesis 3:8-13

These questions serve as watchmen in life.

"The watchmen who go about the city found me; I said, "Have you seen the one I love?" Song of Solomon 3:3

If we grasp how protective He is, and that His protection is truly good, we can better appreciate the many watchmen He places about us. It is consistent through Scripture, and consistent through our lives.

"For as a young man marries a virgin, So shall your sons marry you; And as the bridegroom rejoices over the bride, So shall your God rejoice over you. I have set watchmen on your walls, O Jerusalem; They shall never hold their peace day or night. You who make mention of the LORD, do not keep silent." Isaiah 62:5-6

Our watchmen are: His Word, our consciences, our godly friends and pastors, and anyone and anything pointing us back to the ancient path of truth in the flock, where His presence is unhindered in our lives.

If you feel that you cannot find the Lord, even though you are searching for Him, find a watchman and ask for help, as she does. Very often, when we are confused, others clearly see the blockade. But most people won't point it out unless you ask.

"Scarcely had I passed by them, when I found the one I love. I held him and would not let him go, until I had brought him to the house of my mother, And into the chamber of her who conceived me." Song of Solomon 3:4

He really isn't hard to find! He didn't suffer only to play games with us! But He is, at times, testing our sincerity.

"I have not spoken in secret, In a dark place of the earth; I did not say to the seed of Jacob, 'Seek Me in vain'; I, the LORD, speak righteousness, I declare things that are right." Isaiah 45:19

"When I found the one I love, I held him and would not let him go." Song of Solomon 3:4

His absence is sobering!

There were three years of married life where I allowed what could have been a healthy friendship to morph into codependency. Subtle changes, little foxes. Gradually, I began to need more and more contact with her and with that came a sneaking jealousy of anyone who received her affection. It wasn't the lesbian experience of my past, so I was distressed. These were new and turbulent waters for me, and I didn't know how to navigate.

One by one, watchmen spoke up: *I believe you when you say it's not the sin of your past. But something isn't right, either. You're not free.* They were like voices on a radio station slightly out of tune. I heard them, but I couldn't quite make out what they were saying.

Their prayers were saws slashing at the chains, and after three years, finally, they broke.

He offers the garden we lost in deception
The same fruits, the free will to choose
The lushness, the richness beyond comprehension
The freedom to gain or to lose

And though we are wiser, we are not quite tamed
Forbidden fruit still seem so sweet
But we want to be pure; we do get ashamed
Of kisses of poisoned deceit

Still we hear the seducing shadows call
And dusk is as lethal as night
He offers real colors, real love – it all
When we choose to walk in the light

And when I was sober again, looking at my incredible husband, who had prayed and waited for me as had my incredible Savior, I clutched them both and wouldn't let go. It's been 10 years, and the memory is still such a sting to me that I never, ever want to return.

> "Behold, I am coming quickly! Hold fast what you have, that no one may take your crown. He who overcomes, I will make him a pillar in the temple of My God, and he shall go out no more. I will write on him the name of My God and the name of the city of My God, the New Jerusalem, which comes down out of heaven from My God. And I will write on him My new name. "He who has an ear, let him hear what the Spirit says to the churches." Revelation 3:11-13

"My mother, and into the chamber of her who conceived me," Song of Solomon 3:4, refers to the church and to those who led her to Christ. It's the safe place to retreat and hold on to Him. What He established at first remains true forever: follow the footsteps of the flock.

A pastor, who had been in Chinese prison five times for his faith, exhorted me, *The strongest sheep is in danger outside the flock. The weakest lamb is safe inside the flock. Remain in the flock. The wolf attacks those outside.*

"Thus says the LORD: 'Stand in the ways and see, And ask for the old paths, where the good way is, And walk in it; Then you will find rest for your souls." Jeremiah 6:16

SEARCH ME, O GOD, AND KNOW MY HEART.

- *When You look at my life, what do You see in my hand?*

- *Who are the watchmen in my life?*

- *Am I protected in the flock, or am I in danger on the outside?*

- *Lord, I never want to awaken alone in the shadows again. Please, strengthen the watchmen to speak up when I need warning. Give me ears to hear. Make me a courageous watchman for others, as I commit to live inside the flock, and deepen my understanding of how vital that is.*

DAY 11
Valiance in the Night

God's angels often protect his servants from
potential enemies. - Billy Graham[52]

SONG OF SOLOMON 3:6-11

"Who is this coming out of the wilderness like pillars of smoke, Perfumed with myrrh and frankincense,
with all the merchant's fragrant powders? Behold,
it is Solomon's couch, with sixty valiant men around
it, of the valiant of Israel. They all hold swords,
being expert in war. Every man has his sword on his
thigh Because of fear in the night. Of the wood of
Lebanon Solomon the King Made himself a palanquin: He made its pillars of silver, Its support of

gold, Its seat of purple, its interior paved with love by the daughters of Jerusalem. Go forth, O daughters of Zion, and see King Solomon with the crown with which his mother crowned him on the day of his wedding, the day of the gladness of his heart."

LITERARY TREASURES

The reference to *out of the wilderness* (v.6) *is, since the time of the Mosaic deliverance out of Egypt, an emblem of the transition from bondage to freedom, from humiliation to glory.*[53] *Like pillars of smoke* (v.6), or literally *columns* of smoke invokes the memory of how the Lord led the bewildered Israelites with the pillar of smoke by day and fire by night (Exodus 14:20), *and the pillars of smoke ascending from the altars of incense and of atonement; so Jesus Christ's righteousness, atonement, and ever-living intercession.*[54] "Let my prayer be set before You as incense, The lifting up of my hands as the evening sacrifice. Psalm 141:2

Myrrh and frankincense (v.6) were among the three gifts presented to infant Jesus by the wise men. Unlike Frankincense which is sweet, Myrrh has a bitter taste to it. Myrrh was mostly used to embalm the dead because it had a preservative property. It was also used as perfume, an ingredient of holy ointments mentioned in Exodus. Frankincense was part of the grain offering, which was first mentioned in Exodus 29 as part of the Passover. Repeatedly, when

Frankincense is mentioned, it comes with the appositive, **A sweet aroma to the Lord**. "He shall bring it to Aaron's sons, the priests, one of whom shall take from it his handful of fine flour and oil with all the frankincense. And the priest shall burn it as a memorial on the altar, an offering made by fire, a sweet aroma to the LORD." Leviticus 2:2

Pillars of smoke refers back to His leading them through the wilderness after coming out of Egypt. She has been in a wilderness of her own, but now she can see His pillar again. How much better to be with Him in the wilderness than a slave in Egypt!

COME, FILL THE GAP

Who is this God who meets us in the wilderness? When we left Egypt with nothing familiar to guide us and a slave mentality squeezing our spirits, He was there, guiding, providing, and training us in freedom.

The days and nights when we forget who we are, lost in the wilderness of stress and fear and hormones, He is equally there, ever-present, ever kind, ever gentle, turning our faces back to His majesty. He who first turned our bondage into freedom, never, ever stops. It is who He is.

Gold, Frankincense, and Myrrh, were His welcome gifts into this world (Matthew 2:11), and they are all part of His appearing here, coming out of the wilderness. Embrace the bitter myrrh along the way, remembering that He was born to die for you that your incense might rise freely. Let your slave clothes remain in the desert, as you move closer to your Promised Land. Inhale the frankincense of His presence with you.

Who do the voices in your life tell you that He is? Who do your experiences tell you He is? It matters to Him. As He asked the disciples, "Who do men say that I, the Son of Man, am?...But who do you say that I am?"[55] He is asking us. The landscapes of our hearts and thoughts are entirely visible to Him, but sometimes they are darkened to our view by shadows of untruth.

"For He Himself has said, 'I WILL NEVER LEAVE YOU NOR FORSAKE YOU.' So we may boldly say: "THE LORD IS MY HELPER; I WILL NOT FEAR. WHAT CAN MAN DO TO ME?" Hebrews 13: 5-6

"Behold, it is Solomon's couch, with sixty valiant men around it, of the valiant of Israel. They all hold swords, being expert in war. Every man has his sword on his thigh because of fear in the night." Song of Solomon 3:7-8

Solomon's couch (v.7) is likened to Jesus' body, that which carries Him to the world. *His body, literally, guarded by a definite number of angels, threescore–angels* (Matthew 26:53)...*from the wilderness* (Matthew 4:1,11), *and continually* (Luke 2:13; Luke 22:43; Acts 1:10-11); *just as six hundred thousand of Israel guarded the Lord's tabernacle* (Numbers 2:17-32).[56]

These valiant warriors with swords, experts in war come *because of the fear in the night.*

The fact that they arrive at the scene after her struggle in the shadows, reminds me of Jesus in the desert after His baptism. It was after he had resisted the grueling temptations, solely using the Word of God, our very strongest Watchman, that angels came and ministered to Him. While Matthew's account mentions the ministering angels (4:11), Luke's ends with the ominous "And when the devil had ended all the temptation, he departed from him for a season." (4:13)

He always returns for a season, and we are wise to accept the fact that we are at war, whether we like it or not. There is no opting out, waving the white flag. We march under the Lord's banner of love, and in the real realm, until the devil is finally locked up. Love and conflict are tangled together in a battle for your soul.

"And do not fear those who kill the body but cannot kill the soul. But rather fear Him who is able to destroy both soul and body in hell." Matthew 10:28

"For I am jealous for you with godly jealousy. For I have betrothed you to one husband, that I may present you as a chaste virgin to Christ. But I fear, lest somehow, as the serpent deceived Eve by his craftiness, so your minds may be corrupted from the simplicity that is in Christ." 2 Corinthians 11:2-3

These warriors are here to help protect the simplicity of the Gospel. There is so much craft and deception in the lucrative Christian market place, targeting your money and your simplicity in Christ. There's a divisive undertone of **Unless you pray this way or fast this way, it doesn't count. How to get what you want from God.** Most of it plays to the specific spirit of our time:

> "But know this, that in the last days perilous times will come: For men will be lovers of themselves, lovers of money, boasters, proud, blasphemers, disobedient to parents, unthankful, unholy, unloving, unforgiving, slanderers, without self-control, brutal, despisers of good, traitors, headstrong, haughty, lovers of pleasure rather than lovers of God, having a form of godliness but denying its power. And from such people turn away! For of this sort are those who creep into households and make captives of gullible women loaded down with sins, led away by various lusts, always learning and never able to come to the knowledge of the truth." 2 Timothy 3:1-7

Thus warn both Jesus and Paul. Our goal is not knowledge without change. Our goal is to learn the truth that we might live it! So that we live in His embrace and not in the self-seeking, self-destructive harlot embrace of our culture and our time. He rescued us from a slimy pit, but we still live among thorns and we are not impervious!

But we are not alone! His beauty, His riches and His protection are completely ours when we are in His will.

"Because you have made the LORD, who is my refuge, Even the Most High, your dwelling place, no evil shall befall you, nor shall any plague come near your dwelling; for He shall give His angels charge over you, to keep you in all your ways." Psalm 91:9-11

Just remain in His dwelling place under His banner of love. That is the battle-plan: Abide!

"Of the wood of Lebanon Solomon the King made himself a palanquin: He made its pillars of silver, its support of gold, its seat of purple, its interior paved with love by the daughters of Jerusalem." Song of Solomon 3:9-10

From the strong, fragrant cedar wood, known to dispel moth and decay, our servant King made a palanquin or a chariot (same root word) to carry us out of the wilderness. Reflecting the purity of His Word are its pillars of silver, (Psalm 12:6); reminding of the preciousness of tested faith is its support of gold (1 Peter 1:7); assuring of His constant mercy, new every morning is the royal, purple seat.

Envision this amazing palanquin, inviting you to rest on His mercy with the Prince of Peace himself. When your faith is tested, seek support in the fiery, purified gold. The purple mercy seat is not only available; it is welcoming you. You do not have to rely on visualizing, as so many false shepherds would have you; you hold it in your hands every time you search His Living Word.

Climb into this chariot; it is paved with love. And then...

"Go forth, O daughters of Zion, and see King Solomon with the crown with which his mother crowned him on the day of his wedding, the day of the gladness of his heart." Song of Solomon 3:11

Go forth! He has shown you His majesty, He has brought along His warriors, and He is preparing for the wedding. Now, like the wise virgins in Matthew 25, who took enough oil with them so their lamps wouldn't go out, do likewise. Let the gladness from His heart spark in yours.

"I will greatly rejoice in the LORD, My soul shall be joyful in my God; For He has clothed me with the garments of salvation, He has covered me with the robe of righteousness, As a bridegroom decks himself with ornaments, And as a bride adorns herself with her jewels." Isaiah 61:10

SEARCH ME, O GOD, AND KNOW MY HEART.

* *In the wilderness, do I perceive Your beauty or grumble like the Israelites?*

* *Do I seek Your shelter or disregard the fear in the night?*

- *What does it mean for me to have oil in my lamp, as I wait for Your return?*

- *As I embrace Your invitation to Your mercy seat, Lord I lay down these burdens:*

- *Oh, Lord You are beautiful! Let Your face be all I seek, and may I see Your love for me reflected in Your eyes. Hold me till my heart finds rest.*

DAY 12
None Is Barren

"He has made everything beautiful in its time. Also He has put eternity in their hearts..." Ecclesiastes 3:11

There's so much symbolism in Song of Solomon, and I as I've already made clear: I'm no scholar. I'm just a lover, so hungry and thirsty for His Word's living Water that I try to wring and wrench every life-giving drop out of it. Trembling with the fear of the Lord, I pray to convey His intention for you.

I strive to simply remind you of what you already know. These truths are woven into our DNA. Little children know them. That's why fairytales exist in every culture, stories of damsels in distress and knights in shining armour. These are echoes of the truth. That is why Disney is so successful, and parents are willing to pay fortunes to have their daughters meet and dress like a Disney princess. It's the closest we come to a visual experience of what we intuitively know to be true. Jesus is our knight, and we are damsels awaiting rescue. The eternity in our hearts recognizes and responds to commercialized fairy tales.

With its sweeping, folksy accordion, rousing gypsy guitar, and heart wrenching female vocal, one of my dearly cherished songs is The Flute Behind the Wall, by Savage Rose. My friend, who does not believe in Jesus, wrote it on a hot summer night in Copenhagen.

The windows were open as she lay in the grass under the black roof of night. In the midst of the city noise, a hauntingly sweet flute played somewhere behind a wall. She, as every human being with eternity in heart, longed for the wall to fall, for the consummation of this indefinable oneness with whomever played that flute – the way we all, deepest down, long for the ideal oneness with each other. It is woven into the fabric of our souls. Since the Tower of Babel, humanity has labored to achieve this benefit without the glue Who makes us One. Without Him, in Whom the entire universe is held together, these illusions of utopia deteriorate into societies needing barbed wire and armed guards, as so many totalitarian experiments built on this idealism bear witness.

This is how Jesus prayed for oneness:

> "Now I am no longer in the world, but these are in the world, and I come to You. Holy Father, keep through Your name those whom You have given Me, that they may be one as We are." (John 17:11) "And for their sakes I sanctify Myself, that they also may be sanctified by the truth. I do not pray for these alone, but also for those who will believe in Me through their word; that they all may be one, as You, Father, are in Me, and I in You; that they also may be one in Us, that the world may believe that You sent Me. And the glory which You gave Me I have given them, that they may be one just as We are one: I in them, and You in Me; that they may be made perfect in one, and that the world may know that You have sent Me, and have loved them as You have loved Me." (John 17: 19-23)

He must possess us, for us to be one, as He and the Father are one, and we must be sanctified by the truth.

I pray this Song of Solomon will be like a beautiful flute from Heaven, calling us into a deeper, purer oneness.

Why is it that so many of us find ourselves repeatedly in mangled relationships? There are tensions and unmet expectations because I want others to be more for me than they are able to be or desire to be or ought to be. And they want the same from me.

I promise more than I can deliver, because I just want to be loved or liked, and I am confused about what I should give, should expect from my friends, my family, my church, my God....

We are desperate for validation! We are created for validation!

"A satisfied soul loathes the honeycomb, but to a hungry soul every bitter thing is sweet." Proverbs 27:7

Except the very last verse, the entire fourth chapter of Song of Solomon is His description of us. He wants our soul to be so satisfied that we loathe the sweetness of the false, so that what's bitter doesn't seem sweet to us. We are so hungry...He fills the gaps.

SONG OF SOLOMON 4:1-2

"Behold, you are fair, my love! Behold, you are fair! You have dove's eyes behind your veil. Your hair is like a flock of goats, going down from Mount Gilead. Your teeth are like a flock of shorn sheep

which have come up from the washing, every one of which bears twins, and none is barren among them."

LITERARY TREASURES

Doves eyes: The dove was the only bird counted clean for sacrifice, perhaps because it is known for its faithfulness. We will see Him return to comparing to the turtledove - perhaps He even created it to illustrate to us what faithful, committed love looks like. "For since the creation of the world His invisible attributes are clearly seen, being understood by the things that are made." Romans 1:20

"Your hair is like a flock of goats" **The hair of goats in the East is fine like silk. As long hair is her glory, and marks her subjection to man** (1Corinthians 11:6-15), **so the Nazarite's hair marked his subjection and separation unto God.** (Compare Judges 16:17, with 2 Corinthians 6:17; Titus 2:14; 1 Peter 2:9). **Jesus Christ cares for the minutest concerns of His saints.**"[57]

As the hair's dual meaning, so "Your teeth are like a flock of shorn sheep which have come up from the washing" (Song of Solomon 4:2) alludes to the essential mystery of this Song of a husband washing his wife with the Word. "Just as Christ also loved the church and gave Himself for her, that He might sanctify and cleanse her with the washing of water by the word, that He might present her to Himself a glorious church, not having spot or wrinkle or any such thing, but that she should be holy and without blemish. So husbands ought to love their own wives as their own bodies; he who loves his wife loves himself." (Ephesians 5:25b-28) "You are already clean because of the word which I have spoken to you." (John 15:3)

COME, FILL THE GAP

"Behold, you are fair, my love! Behold, you are fair!" Song of Solomon 4:1

By nature we are **blackened by the sun**, but by grace we are so beautiful that He pronounces it twice. Unlike the empty, self-serving flattery of the world, the praise of Jesus Christ has no strings attached and is not intended to puff up, but to truly edify - to satisfy our hunger in the purest possible way. When He praises us, He is glorified, because like the moon reflecting the sun, we have no light of our own; we are simply reflecting His beauty. Again those same words from The Divine Romance resonate:
She is beautiful, she knows that, yet there is no pride. Rather a deep, inward knowing that he is lord of all earth, and she is...his perfect mate. (pg. 51)

From everything I see in Scripture, He desires us erect in our role as His Bride. Not bent under forgiven sins, not puffed up by false illusions - just erect like a sunflower stretching towards the sun.

"You have dove's eyes behind your veil." (Song of Solomon 4:1) This is the second time her eyes are compared with the doves'. It seems His favorite comparison, so I pray we take in what He is so poetically communicating.

The eyes are the mirror of the soul; they are where our true emotions are easiest seen. I have heard that babies without eye contact wither. I know I wither if those I love withhold eye contact from me. Whenever I want to hide my emotions, I avoid eye contact. On the contrary, infatuation provokes the long gaze into each other's eyes.

"Your hair is like a flock of goats." (Song of Solomon 4:1) This simile is an embrace or a marriage vow: her long, silky hair signals her submission to His authority and in the same breath reminds Him of

His responsibility. Every hair on her head is numbered by Him, and nothing can happen to her outside His protective will.

"But the very hairs of your head are all numbered. Do not fear therefore; you are of more value than many sparrows." Matthew 10:30-31

"Your teeth are like a flock of shorn sheep which have come up from the washing, every one of which bears twins, and none is barren among them." (Song of Solomon 4:2) I had a recurring nightmare that all my teeth fell out. I don't want to read too much into it, but when Brita asked me if I was afraid to speak my convictions, and I realized that in certain situations I was too intimidated to stand by my faith, they stopped.

Jesus declares Himself to be the Living Bread (John 6:35) and makes the astounding promise on which my life is built, that whoever comes to Him shall never hunger, and whoever believes in Him shall never thirst. Faith is the tooth by which we eat the bread. Contrast that with the teeth of our time, so similarly described in Proverbs 30:11-16:

> "There is a generation that curses its father, And does not bless its mother. There is a generation that is pure in its own eyes, Yet is not washed from its filthiness. There is a generation - oh, how lofty are their eyes! And their eyelids are lifted up. There is a generation whose teeth are like swords, And whose fangs are like knives, To devour the poor from off the earth, And the needy from among men. The leech has two daughters - Give and Give! There are three things that are never satisfied, Four never say, "Enough!": The grave, The barren womb, The earth that is not satisfied with water - And the fire never says, "Enough!"

"None is barren among them."(Song of Solomon 4:2) The genera-
tion of these last days is a barren one. Literally. Not only are we not
fruitful - we kill the fruit of our wombs - how many million abortions
each year shout to heaven the truth of 2 Timothy 3, that we are
*lovers of ourselves, without self-control, brutal, headstrong, lovers of
pleasure, rather than lovers of God.* Similarly, we abort the fruit of
our spirit. We are toothless, not living the faith and knowledge we
possess.

But He calls us to the opposite:

"But also for this very reason, giving all diligence, add to your faith
virtue, to virtue knowledge, to knowledge self-control, to self-control perseverance, to perseverance godliness, to godliness brotherly kindness, and to brotherly kindness love. For if these things are
yours and abound, you will be neither barren nor unfruitful in the
knowledge of our Lord Jesus Christ." 2 Peter 1:5-8

Whatever we were, we no longer have to be. There is nothing
He won't forgive. If you have in any way committed abortion, let
Him cleanse. If you, like I, have lived the life described in 2 Timothy,
receive His washing. And having received it, move forward in your
justification. Be free. Be fruitful.

"And such were some of you. But you were washed, but you were
sanctified, but you were justified in the name of the Lord Jesus and
by the Spirit of our God." 1 Corinthians 6:11

SEARCH ME, O GOD, AND KNOW MY HEART THROUGH MY EYES.

- *What do You see there?*

- *Search me, O God, and woo me into deeper trust. Am I in any way resisting submission? If so when? Why?*

- *Search me, O God, and wash me in Your complete forgiveness. Any lies that Your forgiveness is not enough, I reject, in Jesus' Name, and I determine to live in Your washed, sanctified, justified truth about me. Make me fruitful for You.*

DAY 13 : NONE IS BARREN

DAY 13

A Strand of Scarlet

Wise men talk because they have something to say;
Fools, because they have to say something. — Plato

SONG OF SOLOMON 4:3-5

"Your lips are like a strand of scarlet, and your mouth is lovely. Your temples behind your veil are like a piece of pomegranate. Your neck is like the tower of David, built for an armory, on which hang a thousand bucklers, all shields of mighty men. Your two breasts are like two fawns, twins of a gazelle, which feed among the lilies."

LITERARY TREASURES

The first mention of lips in the Bible is when Moses is sentient of his shortcomings as a speaker and terrified at the responsibility God is placing on him, "for I am of uncircumcised lips." (Exodus 6:12) Studies show that public speaking is more frightening than death to the vast majority. On the other hand, Proverbs abounds in warnings about flattering or otherwise destructive words. Jesus and James additionally emphasized the connection between lips and holiness. (Matthew 15:11, James 3:2-12)

Symbolizing her faith in God, Rahab's scarlet cord not only saved the lives of her household, it transferred her identity from a people destined for destruction to the very bloodline of Messiah (Matthew 1:5). By the scarlet blood of Jesus, we make the same leap, and that is what purifies our lips.

Pomegranate: the consensus view is that it symbolizes resurrection and eternal life. The seeds, bursting forth from the fruit, are likened to Christ bursting forth from the tomb. Some also suggest that the many seeds in one fruit are a picture of the church. Nature and parables seemed to be Jesus' favorite tools when attempting to convey the kingdom of Heaven to men of dust, so we listen for His voice, His truth in this symbolism.

Breasts (Song of Solomon 4:5) might be understood very practically through nature. Nursing a baby is reserved for fruitful women, no longer children. We will consider this repeated attribute more throughout our journey, but for now, just ponder that breasts are the delight of a lover, as well as life for the infant. So the church is the delight of her Groom and life for her **children**. A commentary offers a different approach: *the bust is left open in Eastern dress. The breastplate of the high priest was made of 'two' pieces, folded one on the other, in which were the Urim and Thummim (lights and perfection). 'Faith and love' are the double breastplate, answering to 'hearing the word' and 'keeping it', in a similar connection with breasts.*[58]

COME, FILL THE GAP

"Your lips are like a strand of scarlet, and your mouth is lovely. Your temples behind your veil are like a piece of pomegranate"(Song of Solomon 4:3). I love His focus on the mouth. From the first kiss, the teeth, now the lips and the whole mouth! We've already considered how much the mouth is something we associate with emotion, hunger, and insecurity. Jesus says it is what determines whether or not we are clean; not what we eat, but what we speak. "For out of the abundance of the heart the mouth speaks." Matthew 12:34

Even without profanity, some people leave a septic stench, no matter what they say. It is the vitriol and acidity of a Jerry Springer show. There's a sense of decay, as rotting relationships are displayed in exchange for fifteen minutes of fame. Disgusted, most of us turn away from it, instinctively wanting out of the gutter. Not only do we know, we feel the truth of the Proverb, "Death and life are in the power of the tongue."

Gossip furnishes a slightly different discomfort. We know it is unacceptable, but somehow we are often more concerned with not being impolite, as we wish to escape the conversation, afraid we cannot do so graciously. But oh, the sting, when the conviction arrives! Do you recollect leaving a situation and suddenly re-hearing your own voice, realizing with brazen clarity that the poisonous words sprang from you? Then it becomes worse, realizing how it not only injures someone's reputation, but also directly hurts their Maker!

Do you know someone whose very presence diffuses a fragrance of grace? My Brita does this so consistently that I am never afraid for her to see the real me, even when I am the most ashamed of myself. Her lips are scarlet; their scent is forgiveness, and they bring life. How much more the Words of Life Himself! When the mud and muck of conviction, embarrassment, and falling short defile, let Him breathe on you and wash you. "If we confess our sins, He is faithful and just to forgive us our sins and to cleanse us from all unrighteousness." I John 1:9

Let Him fill your mouth with laughter, with joy at the freedom of being cleansed. Let a new song rise up from the heart through scarlet lips. "For then I will restore to the peoples a pure language, that they all may call on the name of the LORD, to serve Him with one accord." Zephaniah 3:9

"Let your speech always be with grace, seasoned with salt, that you may know how you ought to answer each one." Colossians 4:6

Oh, Lord, come fill the gap! The spirit is willing, but the flesh is weak! Thank goodness my lips are scarlet; they are covered by His blood. Scarlet was the thread that rescued Rahab, and like her, I am aware of my own filth. There is nothing I repent of as much as words I shouldn't have said! Because He continually reapplies the scarlet color to my lips, my mouth is lovely.

"Therefore by Him let us continually offer the sacrifice of praise to God, that is, the fruit of our lips, giving thanks to His name." Hebrews 13:15

"Your temples behind your veil are like a piece of pomegranate." Song of Solomon 4:3 What I hear is this: Your temples behind your veil or hair (the Hebrew word can mean both) are like a pomegranate; your private thoughts are now in alignment with eternity. It is not for show; it is true in private, behind the veil. You are authentic.

"Your neck is like the tower of David, Built for an armory, on which hang a thousand bucklers, all shields of mighty men." Song of Solomon 4:4 Because of His grace, my neck is no longer stiff, as when I was stubborn; no longer stretched in sinful directions, as when I lived in the flesh; no longer burdened in a legal yoke, for I have taken His easy, light yoke upon me; so my neck is erect in the freedom He died to deliver.

David was a man of war, preceding the reign of Solomon's peace. Like the tower of David, I live in time of war, proceeding the complete reign of the Prince of Peace. Each victory I win is a heavenly trophy, and as I am part of the global church, the eternal Bride, somehow our collective victories, a thousand shields of mighty men, are part of my regalia before Him.

"He who has an ear, let him hear what the Spirit says to the churches." Revelation 2:11

"Your two breasts are like two fawns, twins of a gazelle, which feed among the lilies." Song of Solomon 4:5 "But let us who are of the day be sober, putting on the breastplate of faith and love, and as a helmet the hope of salvation." 1 Thessalonians 5:8

As I read this Song, I keep thinking of the breasts (and they will be addressed more than once) as the very practical life source they are, as we mature from girls into women. They are how He designed us to feed our babies, and His Word refers to this baby milk when describing our initial feeding on His Word:

"Therefore, laying aside all malice, all deceit, hypocrisy, envy, and all evil speaking, as newborn babes, desire the pure milk of the word, that you may grow thereby, if indeed you have tasted that the Lord is gracious." 1Peter 2:1-3

So having tasted that He is gracious, having laid aside the malice Peter lists, we now feed others the pure milk of the Word and help them grow. Fawns and gazelles feed among, not on the lilies. As we'll see later in the Song, the Shepherd feeds His flock among the lilies. She no longer lives among thorns; she is increasingly among the lilies. And as one among the multitude of lilies, I imagine their whiteness morph into the white wedding dress. She is getting ready, and she is now helping others get ready, as well.

SEARCH ME, O GOD, AND KNOW MY HEART

• *O God, make Your praises from this Word be true of me behind my veil to the deepest cell in my being. Let Your resurrection truth be my DNA.*

• *"So I said: "Woe is me, for I am undone!
Because I am a man of unclean
lips, and I dwell in the midst of a
people of unclean lips; for my eyes
have seen the King, The LORD of hosts."
Then one of the seraphim flew to me,
having in his hand a live coal which
he had taken with the tongs from the altar.
And he touched my mouth with it, and said:
"Behold, this has touched your lips; your iniquity is
taken away, and your sin purged." Isaiah 6:5-7*

• *Before anything else, Lord, convict me of unclean speech. Have I offended You with my lips?*

• *Have I hurt or offended anyone else?*

- *Do I in any way hinder authenticity or pretend to be what I am not?*

- *Does my neck need a massage; has it grown stiff or weary or bent?*

- *How mature are my breasts? Are they feeding others Your grace, or has any form of malice stunted their growth?*

- *When you look at my friends, is there the right balance of thorns and lilies?*

- *Bring Your coal, touch my lips, purge my sin. Jesus, Lover of my soul, soak me in Your grace so completely that my neck is erect, my milk is pure, as I prepare for our Wedding.*

Come, Fill the Gap

DAY 14

His Enduring, Assuring Sacrifice

Long before Jesus died He made a great
sacrifice for us; He gave up who He was as
God with all His power and might.[59]

SONG OF SONGS 4:6-7

*"Until the day breaks and the shadows flee
away, I will go my way to the mountain of myrrh
and to the hill of frankincense. You are all
fair, my love, and there is no spot in you."*

LITERARY TREASURES

Consider John Gill's fascinating intuition on *the mountain of myrrh and the hill of frankincense: most of the Jewish writers understand the temple, which was built on mount Moriah (2 Chronicles 3:1), as the place where Abraham offered up his son Isaac. This is where the Lord so frequently in after-ages, appeared unto his people. The temple may be called "the mountain of myrrh and hill of frankincense," in allusion to Moriah, the name of the mountain on which it was built (from the abundance of myrrh which grew upon it). Alternatively, the name may arise because in it was the holy anointing oil, one ingredient in which was "pure myrrh" and also the incense made of "pure frankincense.*[60]

To have *no spot* or be *without spot*, as Scripture more frequently phrases it, is a condition only attainable through the Lamb of God Himself, who was "without spot and blameless." (2 Peter 3:14) We cannot restore our own spiritual virginity:

"Christ also loved the church and gave Himself for her, that He might sanctify and cleanse her with the washing of water by the word, that He might present her to Himself a glorious church, not having spot or wrinkle or any such thing, but that she should be holy and without blemish." Ephesians 5:25-27

COME, FILL THE GAP

"Until the day breaks and the shadows flee away, I will go my way to the mountain of myrrh and to the hill of frankincense." (Song of Solomon 4:6) Do you recognize these words: "Until the day breaks and the shadows flee... go away... mountains..."? These were the words she used to send Him away to the Mountains of Separation. His attention to detail stuns me, how every word we say, every tear we cry, every prayer we sigh, every hair on our head, has His full attention. You may know, but do you grasp in day-to-day life that your prayers are in a golden bowl as incense before His Throne. He who never slumbers or sleeps, hears, sees, feels, understands and remembers everything about you.

> "Now when He had taken the scroll, the four living creatures and the twenty-four elders fell down before the Lamb, each having a harp, and golden bowls full of incense, which are the prayers of the saints." Revelation 5:8

A varying interpretation of **the hill of frankincense** is Calvary, where He offered up Himself, and **the mountain of myrrh is His embalment**. So what is He telling her?

You sent me to the mountains of Separation, but there is a mountain stronger still. I heard every word you said; I know why you said them, and just in case you need to know again - I died for you! "I am with you always, even to the end of the age."(Matthew 28:20) Until the day breaks and the shadows flee away, I am with you.

Perhaps He is assuring her because He senses fragility. There are times when my man perceives something in my eyes or body language, of which I am unaware, signaling to him sadness, dryness - a thirst for tenderness. And as he holds me and assures me that I am his favorite wife (don't worry, I am his only), a tension relaxes, and the water of his love softens dry ground inside me, making it soft and fertile again.

Your Lover never tires of this. He is never distracted or concerned that you might be too needy. You cannot get too close, too dependent, too trusting. The deeper your thirst, the deeper His well. Offer Him your poverty and He will bestow on you His Kingdom. "Blessed are the poor in spirit, for theirs is the kingdom of heaven." Matthew 5:3

Our lavish Lover continues: "You are all fair, my love, and there is no spot in you." Song of Solomon 4:7

This is exactly what He told her in verse 1. Unlike our sophisticated, rushed, get-to-the-point, instant world, He has no difficulty repeating Himself. He is outside of time, nurturing each human heart as if it were the only one. You are His favorite. Not only did He leave heaven behind for your rescue, He tenderly and patiently heals the wounds that caused you to send Him away. The fear to trust His heart, the fear that He would see in you the **darkness from the sun**, the residue of who you used to be, with all these He is intimately acquainted. He knows what's what; He sees you in the light of absolute truth and limitless love. And His love frees you to love Him back.

"Husbands, love your wives, just as Christ also loved the church and gave Himself for her, that He might sanctify and cleanse her with the washing of water by the word, that He might present her to Himself a glorious church, not having spot or wrinkle or any such thing, but that she should be holy and without blemish." (Ephesians 5:25-27) Again borrowing the words of John Gill,

> *He says so of the church, to manifest the exceeding greatness of her beauty, and how much his heart was taken with it, that he, the king, greatly desired it, and delighted to be in her company. To comfort her, banish her doubts and fears, and strengthen her faith; who, seeing her own vileness and sinfulness, and spots and blemishes, might be ready to despond in her mind, and call in question her interest in Christ, and his righteousness; therefore he says, 'Thou art all fair, my love: I do love thee; thou art exceeding fair and beautiful in my eye; all of thee is fair and beautiful; thou art fairer than all others, being adorned with my grace, and clothed with my righteousness.'*[61]

Do not be snared into meditating on your flaws. There is no freedom there. Rather stretch yourself, all that you are, towards His loving light and let His illumination expose and dispose of the sin. In some circles, there's such a focus on our own holiness that we turn our backs on Him in the process of navel-gazing. That was never what He intended; that is not humility. Rather than being concerned with self (whether self-aggrandizing or self-loathing), humility, by the hand of His grace, lifts its gaze out and up.

> Do not imagine that if you meet a really humble man he will be what most people call 'humble' nowadays: he will not be a sort of greasy, smarmy person, who is always telling you that, of course, he is nobody. Probably all you will think about him is that he seemed a cheerful, intelligent chap who took a real interest in what you said to him. If you do dislike him it will be because you feel a little envious of anyone who seems to enjoy life so easily. He will not be thinking about humility: he will not be thinking about himself at all.[62]

He really wants you free! He really is for you. Can you feel the fresh air?

> "What then shall we say to these things? If God is for us, who can be against us? He who did not spare His own Son, but delivered Him up for us all, how shall He not with Him also freely give us all things? Who shall bring a charge against God's elect? It is God who justifies. Who is he who condemns? It is Christ who died, and furthermore is also risen, who is even at the right hand of God, who also makes intercession for us. Who shall separate us from the love of Christ? Shall tribulation, or distress, or persecution, or famine, or nakedness, or peril, or sword? As it is written: 'FOR YOUR SAKE WE ARE KILLED ALL DAY LONG; WE ARE ACCOUNTED AS SHEEP FOR THE SLAUGHTER.' Yet in all these things we are more than conquerors through Him who loved

us. For I am persuaded that neither death nor life, nor angels nor principalities nor powers, nor things present nor things to come, nor height nor depth, nor any other created thing, shall be able to separate us from the love of God which is in Christ Jesus our Lord." Rom 8:31-39

"I can do all things through Christ who strengthens me." Philippians 4:13

SEARCH ME, O GOD, AND KNOW MY HEART

- *Show me if I have any reservation at receiving the fullness of Your love.*

- *Am I still tempted to send You away, so I live my own way?*

- *Am I free from condemnation or under its weight?*

- *Speak to my fragile soul the Words that wash and cleanse. Lift my eyes to the Cross on Calvary and help me grasp its completeness - for me, and for those I love.*

DAY 15

His Invitation

Everybody has to leave, everybody has to leave their home and come back so they can love it again for all new reasons. - Donald Miller[63]

SONG OF SOLOMON 4:8-11

"*Come with me from Lebanon, my spouse, with me from Lebanon. Look from the top of Amana, from the top of Senir and Hermon, from the lions' dens, from the mountains of the leopards. You have ravished my heart, My sister, My spouse; You have ravished my heart with one look of your eyes, with one link of your necklace. How fair is your love, My sister, My spouse! How much better than wine is your love, and the scent of your perfumes than all spices! Your lips, O My spouse, drip as the honeycomb; honey and milk are under your tongue; and the fragrance of your garments is like the fragrance of Lebanon."*

LITERARY TREASURES

Mentioned 70 times in the Old Testament, Lebanon (today the Lebanese Republic) is bordered by Syria to the north and east, and Israel to the south. *The earthy fragrance of the region's cedar trees is unforgettable. King Solomon had these choice trees specially brought down to use in his temple for the Lord centuries ago.*[64] But the mountain range is also dangerously populated by leopards and lions (v. 8). *Now, centuries later, the terrorist group Hezbollah has chosen some of these very same sites to launch their war against Israel.*[65] Amana is a mountain near Damascus; Senir, meaning **pointed** is a summit in Lebanon.

Sister, spouse (v.9) *This title is here first used, as He is soon about to institute the Supper, the pledge of the nuptial union. By the term 'sister', carnal ideas are excluded; the ardor of a spouse's love is combined with the purity of a sister's.* [66]

Honey and milk (v.11) are symbolic of the Promised Land. "So I have come down to deliver them out of the hand of the Egyptians and to bring them up from that land to a good and large land, to a land flowing with milk and honey." (Exodus 3:8) In contrast, "They sharpen their tongues like a serpent; the poison of asps is under their lips." Psalm 140:3

COME, FILL THE GAP

"Come with me from Lebanon, My spouse, with me from Lebanon. Look from the top of Amana, from the top of Senir and Hermon, from the lions' dens, from the mountains of the leopards." Song of Solomon 4:8

Come with me away from the border mountains among the hostile lands north of the Promised land.

When I was so newly saved that my head was spinning and my feet wobbly, I had a sense that I had just jumped over an endless abyss into His arms on the other side. Meeting His eyes on the Cross had given me the courage to attempt the leap; all I could think of was to live in the light of those eyes.

But once I landed and caught my balance, I realized that I was dangerously close to that abyss, dallying around the edge without rail or rope. As a parent beckons a toddler, I sensed Him with outstretched arms calling my name as He gently coaxed me away from the edge, deeper and deeper into His protection.

That is the image I see here – that is His invitation.

Senir was infested by devouring lions and swift leopards. In contrast, in His land, "No lion shall be there, nor shall any ravenous beast go up on it; it shall not be found there. But the redeemed shall walk there, and the ransomed of the LORD shall return, and come to Zion with singing, with everlasting joy on their heads. They shall obtain joy and gladness, and sorrow and sighing shall flee away." Isaiah 35: 9-10

"Listen, O daughter, Consider and incline your ear; forget your own people also, and your father's house; so the King will greatly desire your beauty; because He is your Lord, worship Him." Psalm 45:10-11

Sometimes, for seasons or for life, He calls us to leave loved ones behind as we follow Him where only the redeemed can go. For most of us, this is the most painful part of following Him. But it is necessary. If you stay too long in the border country, the pull from the other side strengthens.

In retrospect, I wonder if I did it well when I followed Him to a land where none of my friends were willing to go. The pain of knowing they didn't understand still stings. Could I have chosen better words? Probably. Could I have somehow been more gentle? I don't think so. I would have been like the disciple, mentioned by both Matthew and Luke, whose response to Jesus' **Follow Me** was, **First let me bury my father.** Following Him with virtually no strings to the old land enabled me to quickly and purely drink in His water and milk. He had more access to me, because they had less.

> "But what things were gain to me, these I have counted loss for Christ. Yet indeed I also count all things loss for the excellence of the knowledge of Christ Jesus my Lord, for whom I have suffered the loss of all things, and count them as rubbish, that I may gain Christ and be found in Him, not having my own righteousness, which is from the law, but that which is through faith in Christ, the righteousness which is from God by faith; that I may know Him and the power of His resurrection, and the fellowship of His sufferings, being conformed to His death, if, by any means, I may attain to the resurrection from the dead. Not that I have already attained, or am already perfected; but I press on, that I may lay hold of that for which Christ Jesus has also laid hold of me. Brethren, I do not count myself to have appre-hended; but one thing I do, forgetting those things which are behind and reaching forward to those things which are ahead, I press toward the goal for

the prize of the upward call of God in Christ Jesus."
Philippians 3:7-14

Press forward toward the goal for the prize of the upward call of
God in Christ Jesus. He is worth it! "Come with Me....with Me," He
invites you in this passionately redeeming Song (4:8).

"Then Peter said, 'See, we have left all and followed You.' So He said
to them, 'Assuredly, I say to you, there is no one who has left house
or parents or brothers or wife or children, for the sake of the kingdom of God, who shall not receive many times more in this present
time, and in the age to come eternal life.'" Luke 18:28-30

"You have ravished my heart, My sister, My spouse; you have ravished My heart with one look of your eyes, with one link of your
necklace." Song of Solomon 4:9

This is the first time He combines those two titles, sister and spouse.
It almost sounds incestuous - how can we be both? Yet we are:

"For your Maker is your husband, The LORD of hosts is His name;
and your Redeemer is the Holy One of Israel; He is called the God
of the whole earth." (Isaiah 54:5) "For whoever does the will of God
is My brother and My sister and mother." Mark 3:35

It is nearly impossible for us to grasp a love that is so white-hot pure
and so vast that it contains all the different kinds of love we are
familiar with and more, with no carnality whatsoever. With my man,
sometimes I am more like a sister, and others times more like a lover,
but not both at the same time. But that is because I am so limited;
even one of those at a time is shallow and flawed in me.

"With one look of your eyes..." (Song of Solomon 4:9) One look,
one love, one leap into His arms, every one a sinner saved...

"I say to you that likewise there will be more joy in heaven over one sinner who repents than over ninety-nine just persons who need no repentance." Luke 15:7

> "With one link of your necklace" (Song of Solomon 4:9) "You shall also be a crown of glory in the hand of the LORD, And a royal diadem in the hand of your God. You shall no longer be termed Forsaken, nor shall your land any more be termed Desolate; But you shall be called Hephzibah, and your land Beulah; for the LORD delights in you, and your land shall be married. For as a young man marries a virgin, so shall your sons marry you; And as the bridegroom rejoices over the bride, so shall your God rejoice over you. I have set watchmen on your walls, O Jerusalem; they shall never hold their peace day or night." Isaiah 62:3-6

Heaven is fashioned in jewels and gold. In all the Old Testament references I recall, His hand is placing jewelry on her. I can only guess that they are the treasures we store up - what He finds precious in us:

> "Do not let your adornment be merely outward - arranging the hair, wearing gold, or putting on fine apparel - rather let it be the hidden person of the heart, with the incorruptible beauty of a gentle and quiet spirit, which is very precious in the sight of God." 1 Peter 3:3-4

"How fair is your love, my sister, my spouse! How much better than wine is your love, and the scent of your perfumes than all spices!" Song of Solomon 4:10

Again He repeats her words back to her, praises she lavished on Him early on: "Because of the fragrance of your good ointments, Your name is ointment poured forth." Song of Solomon 1:3

Again, He echoes her love, savors her praise - Oh that we could fathom how much our praises matter.

"Your lips, O my spouse, drip as the honeycomb; honey and milk are under your tongue; and the fragrance of your garments is like the fragrance of Lebanon." Song of Solomon 4:11

> "Give ear, O heavens, and I will speak; And hear, O earth, the words of my mouth. Let my teaching drop as the rain, my speech distill as the dew, as raindrops on the tender herb, And as showers on the grass. For I proclaim the name of the LORD: Ascribe greatness to our God." Deuteronomy 32:1-3

Saturate me in Your Water, that my speech would drop like rain, bringing life to those around me and joy to Your heart. Savor, Lord, whatever authentic praises my soul sings to You, and let my tongue be one of milk and honey from the Promised Land.

"Pleasant words are like a honeycomb, sweetness to the soul and health to the bones." Proverbs 16:24

"My son, eat honey because it is good, and the honeycomb which is sweet to your taste; so shall the knowledge of wisdom be to your soul; if you have found it, there is a prospect, and your hope will not be cut off." Proverbs 24:13-14

> "I will heal their backsliding, I will love them freely, for My anger has turned away from him. I will be like the dew to Israel; he shall grow like the lily, and lengthen his roots like Lebanon. His branches shall

spread; his beauty shall be like an olive tree, and his fragrance like Lebanon. Those who dwell under his shadow shall return; they shall be revived like grain, and grow like a vine. Their scent shall be like the wine of Lebanon." Hosea 14:4-7

SEARCH ME, O GOD, AND KNOW MY HEART.

- *May my life be an ambrosial fragrance to You. Let honey pour from my lips as I praise you now.*

DAY 16
A Garden Enclosed

*Remember that children, marriages, and
flower gardens reflect the kind of care
they get. - H. Jackson Brown, Jr.*[67]

SONG OF SOLOMON 4:12-15

*"A garden enclosed is my sister, my spouse, a spring shut
up, a fountain sealed. Your plants are an orchard of
pomegranates with pleasant fruits, fragrant henna with
spikenard, spikenard and saffron, Calamus and cinnamon, with all trees of frankincense, myrrh and aloes,
with all the chief spices - A fountain of gardens, a
well of living waters, and streams from Lebanon.*

LITERARY TREASURES

Charles Spurgeon wrote:

> After the creation of the universe and of man, God planted a garden. A garden is neither a common ground nor ground for the planting of just any old thing, but for the production of something of beauty and pleasure. He is looking for flowers and blossoms which are to be gathered as something beautiful and exotic.
>
> She does not exist for herself but for the pleasure and satisfaction of her bridegroom. She is not merely a common garden but 'a garden enclosed' which includes a 'spring shut up, a fountain sealed.' It is not a public garden for any passerby. The seal showed someone owned it.
>
> Every open vessel (or well) which has no covering on it is unclean (polluted, contaminated) and is unfit for drinking. An open vessel is for public usage and is exposed to every kind of disease and adverse influence. What is not wholly set apart for the Lord Jesus alone is open to almost anything. If only believers would be enclosed more than they are, if their coverings were a little more fitting – the Lord's work would be much easier. An enclosed garden or spring is clean and pure and set aside to be refreshment for the Lord and His people. [68]

COME, FILL THE GAP

"A garden enclosed is my sister, my spouse, a spring shut up, a fountain sealed." (Song of Solomon 4:12) More than any other verse in the Bible, this one has preserved me though all kinds of seasons. It has been my retreat, my protection, and my reservoir of beauty. An extrovert with voices uncounted calling out to me, this oasis has been the filter sifting the demands from outside the garden, as well as the perpetual press of my own meddling desires.

We are sealed with the Holy Spirit. Nevertheless, His ownership is visible to the spirit world, but not necessarily the physical realm. We see in Revelation that the angels declare whose we are, but sometimes we ourselves are confused. We want to be fruitful, but the needs are more than we can meet. We want to be loving, but not controlled or codependent. Sometimes among believers, there's the notion that the more we work ourselves to death in His vineyard, the more spiritual we are.

More than once I've sat with a disgruntled woman, disappointed that I didn't answer her phone call. "What if I really needed you?" As a pastor's wife, it seems there is no limit to the list of what that title should entail. I am a home schooling mother of two teens, as well as a teacher in an academically ambitious school. I am profoundly grateful for all of it — it's a big life, and it's mine.

NO! It is His!

Before anything or anyone else, every fiber of my being belongs to the One who said to me, *Live!* I am not a public park where dogs walk and kids run loose and nobody really cares. I am His enclosed garden. I rest in that and retreat to that, because I know HE can fill every gap in those who look to me expectantly. He does not take my daughter ice skating, but only He can meet her deepest needs.

Inside my enclosure with Him, my blood pressure recedes, so its rush doesn't deafen my ears. Inside my enclosure with Him, the unessential is pruned from the essential. Order and simplicity return. Inside my enclosure with Him, I remember whose I am, and I exhale into His care.

I pray for you:

May you discover the unique beauty of the garden He tends with You. May you be free to not fill every gap that clamors for attention, but in the quietness of His protection establish His boundaries. May you know that they are pleasant and that His inheritance for you is good.

"O LORD, You are the portion of my inheritance and my cup; You maintain my lot. The lines have fallen to me in pleasant places; Yes, I have a good inheritance." Psalm 16:5-6

"The LORD will guide you continually, and satisfy your soul in drought, and strengthen your bones; you shall be like a watered garden, and like a spring of water, whose waters do not fail." Isaiah 58:11

There is a place in His garden
I rarely come to enjoy;
The tenderness there is so naked,
The silence I fear to destroy.

There is a depth in his presence
I hardly dare to believe;
For in his heart lives the essence
Of all I could hope to achieve.

He shows me His Kingdom's delights,
Where future kisses times of old,
Where freedom kisses sacrifice,
Where nothing more can trap my soul.

He shows me the eternal flames.
They burn as from his agony –
His grief - when I hold on to shame
For which He died to set me free.

There is a victorious Promise
Inviting me into its dance;
There, beyond my shy hesitation
I find life itself in His hands.

Let's retire into the garden to admire the work of His hands:

"Your plants are an orchard of pomegranates with pleasant fruits, fragrant henna with spikenard, spikenard and saffron, Calamus and cinnamon, with all trees of frankincense, myrrh and aloes, with all the chief spices - A fountain of gardens, a well of living waters, and streams from Lebanon." Song of Solomon 4:13-15

Rather than dissect each fruit and spice, just take in the teeming bounty. This is a symphony of beauty sounding all the way from Eden and cajoling our souls towards the New Earth. Savor the pictures and associations - and then try to take it in: this is how He sees you!

"They are abundantly satisfied with the fullness of Your house, and You give them drink from the river of Your pleasures. For with You is the fountain of life; in Your light we see light." Psalm 36:8-9

"There is a river whose streams shall make glad the city of God, The holy place of the tabernacle of the Most High. God is in the midst of her, she shall not be moved; God shall help her, just at the break of dawn." Psalm 46:4-5

"And he showed me a pure river of water of life, clear as crystal, proceeding from the throne of God and of the Lamb. In the middle of its street, and on either side of the river, was the tree of life, which bore twelve fruits, each tree yielding its fruit every month. The leaves of the tree were for the healing of the nations. And there shall be no more curse, but the throne of God and of the Lamb shall be in it, and His servants shall serve Him. They shall see His face, and His name shall be on their foreheads." Revelation 22:1-4

SEARCH ME, O GOD, AND KNOW MY HEART.

- *Where might I find the quiet realm with You?*

- *Show me the fullness of Your house in my life.*

- *Lord, describe my garden to me.*

- *I immerse in Your Living Water; I take in the beauty by faith; I will bear Your seal wisely.*

DAY 17 : A GARDEN ENCLOSED

DAY 17

Invitation

*If you find in yourself a desire which no earthly
thing can satisfy, the logical conclusion must be that
you are made for another world. - C. S. Lewis*[69]

SONG OF SOLOMON 4:16-5:1

"Awake, O north wind, And come, O south!
Blow upon my garden, that its spices may flow
out. Let my beloved come to his garden and eat its
pleasant fruits. I have come to my garden, my sister, my spouse; I have gathered my myrrh with my
spice; I have eaten my honeycomb with my honey; I
have drunk my wine with my milk. Eat, O friends!
Drink, yes, drink deeply, O beloved ones!"

LITERARY TREASURES

Awake also means **arise** and is thus a resonance of His summons to her in chapter 2, verse 10. Increasingly, they are adopting the terms of intimate friendship. **Blow** denotes **blow with the breath...to fan... to kindle**[70] It is the invitation accepted for all believers when "He breathed on them, and said to them, 'Receive the Holy Spirit.'" John 20:22

I prefer the word **fragrant** to **odor** from this 1871 commentary, because pleasure is penetrating the heart of this highest song. She, symbolizing every Spirit-filled Christian, is the delicate, enclosed garden where the fruit and the fragrances are His. "By this My Father is glorified, that you bear much fruit; so you will be My disciples." John 15:8

COME, FILL THE GAP

Overflowing and saturated in His affirmation and protection, we delight in the abundance of the enclosed garden and the brisk living waters.

Do you know the feeling of dragging yourself, weary and worn from a dull as dishwater life, with worries and details into worship or into His presence? Perhaps a good friend or a special song is how He takes you to where you know all is well. You rest in Him; you are willing to do anything for Him; in that presence nothing else matters. That is why we worship — because it is not an escape; it is a return to reality.

In those moments we invite His Spirit to have free reign: "Awake, O north wind, And come, O south! Blow upon my garden." (Song of Solomon 4:16) In those moments, we welcome anything from Him;

we might even long for rebuke; anything! In those moments we lust for His untamed freedom.

"The wind blows where it wishes, and you hear the sound of it, but cannot tell where it comes from and where it goes. So is everyone who is born of the Spirit." John 3:8

The north wind is cold, even harsh. The howling winds by the North Sea where I grew up cut through layers of clothing; they are brutal, but they leave you with flushed cheeks, refreshed and awake. The Holy Spirit, the Spirit of truth, has that effect:

> "And when He has come, He will convict the world of sin, and of righteousness, and of judgment: of sin, because they do not believe in Me; of righteousness, because I go to My Father and you see Me no more; of judgment, because the ruler of this world is judged. I still have many things to say to you, but you cannot bear them now. However, when He, the Spirit of truth, has come, He will guide you into all truth; for He will not speak on His own authority, but whatever He hears He will speak; and He will tell you things to come. He will glorify Me, for He will take of what is Mine and declare it to you." John 16:8-14

When His north wind blows through, gradually guiding you into truth, as you can handle it, He will do so in the authority of your Lover. And whatever He shows you is for the purpose of glorifying Jesus. Sometimes, when we are open in worship, we welcome that. Other times, diluted by pride or stress, we hide in self-protection from the very wind that would bring refreshment and freedom.

Of course, I much prefer the south wind, the Helper who comforts when I feel orphaned. He is still truth, but He is warm.

"And I will pray the Father, and He will give you another Helper, that He may abide with you forever - the Spirit of truth, whom the world cannot receive, because it neither sees Him nor knows Him; but you know Him, for He dwells with you and will be in you. I will not leave you orphans; I will come to you." John 14:16-18

"That its spices may flow out. Let my beloved come to his garden and eat its pleasant fruits." Song of Solomon 4:16

Do you know the feeling of being so satiated by Him that all you long for is for His fragrance to flow out from your garden – for His beauty to radiate – and for HIM to just enjoy who you are in Him? That is the deepest intimacy, and it's almost painful, because in the yearning there is awareness that it's not fully satisfied. We still inhabit an earthly tent, and this union is of another world. We can't stay in this emotion – but it's what we're meant for. It is a bittersweet appetizer for the banquet, a reminder that soon and very soon the embrace will be unbroken, and the *realities* of bills and traffic won't seem so real.

It requires these purifying winds of the Holy Spirit to let our spices blow out. He makes us more US, more ourselves, than we could ever be otherwise. And it is in our authenticity that His fragrance flows out. We don't pretend. We are. We don't attempt to control the winds or the spices; we are not preoccupied with managing image. These are the times He is most visibly transcending us and reaching through us to those around us.

> "I have come to my garden, my sister, my spouse;
> I have gathered my myrrh with my spice; I have eaten
> my honeycomb with my honey; I have drunk my wine
> with my milk. Eat, O friends! Drink, yes, drink deeply,
> O beloved ones!" Song of Solomon 5:1

Again He echoes her words; He immediately responds to her invitation, but this time He adds His own details:

Eat, O friends! Drink, yes, drink deeply, O beloved ones!

He responds again with deep assurance: I am enjoying your fruits, and now I'm inviting others to enjoy them. His love for us is never meant to be lived in a vacuum! Yes, there's the enclosed garden where He alone is the Gardener — but He always, always intends fruit. He always intends for His blessing TO us to become a blessing THROUGH us!

"Then the Angel of the LORD called to Abraham a second time out of heaven, and said: 'By Myself I have sworn, says the LORD, because you have done this thing, and have not withheld your son, your only son - blessing I will bless you, and multiplying I will multiply your descendants as the stars of the heaven and as the sand which is on the seashore; and your descendants shall possess the gate of their enemies. In your seed all the nations of the earth shall be blessed, because you have obeyed My voice.'" Genesis 22:15-18

This song is progressive. From the first longing for His kiss to the deepest commitment in the last verse, it moves forward and has the ups and downs of our humanity.

In chapter 3, she sent Him away, because she wanted to dance with sin.

In Chapter 4, they are reunited, and He is pouring into her deep affirmation and restoration. And she is responding with the deepest surrender, and all seems well.

But in chapter 5, He takes her up on her offer and invites her further into ministry.

SEARCH ME, O GOD, AND KNOW MY HEART

- *Am I hiding from your winds in any way?*

- *Am I aware that the pleasant fruits in my life are Yours, or are weeds of pride choking them?*

- *Tell me about Your invitation to follow You further...*

DAY 18

Hesitation

If you gain, you gain all. If you lose, you lose nothing. Wager then, without hesitation, that He exists - Blaise Pascal.[71]

SONG OF SOLOMON 5:2-3

"I sleep, but my heart is awake; it is the voice of my beloved! He knocks, saying, 'Open for me, my sister, my love, My dove, my perfect one; For my head is covered with dew, My locks with the drops of the night...I have taken off my robe; how can I put it on again? I have washed my feet; How can I defile them?'"

LITERARY TREASURES

Heart is used (figuratively) very widely for the feelings, the will, and even the intellect; likewise for the centre of anything[72] and *awake* denotes the idea of opening the eyes.[73] It is a state Cicero calls *semi-somni*.[74] John Gill enlightens, *First, she acknowledges that she was asleep. 'I sleep.' This is not the dead sleep of sin, in whom all unconverted persons are; nor that judicial slumber, which God suffers to fall upon some; but such an one, which though displeasing to Christ and unbecoming the believer, yet is consistent with a principle of grace. The church here was not so fast asleep, but she could hear, know, and distinguish the voice of Christ; her sleep is much the same with that of the wise virgins, who all slumbered and slept, as well as the foolish, and yet had oil in their lamps, which they had not.*[75]

Captivating in its clear reference to the beloved believer, affirming once again that this love song is from Jesus, our Living Word, the Hebrew word here translated **perfect one** is defined as **complete; usually (morally) pious…gentle, dear.**[76] The King James Version translates it **undefiled.**

John Gill compares her response to that of chapter 2, verse 17 , "… in there she was upon her bed indeed, but not asleep; there she was seeking after her beloved; but here he is seeking her, and entreating her in the most kind and affectionate manner to arise, and let him in; there she of her own accord arose and sought him in the streets and broad ways; but here she continues in this sleepy and lazy condition, notwithstanding the pressing instances and powerful arguments which he made use of."[77]

COME, FILL THE GAP

The center of her being is awake; she is aware of what He wants. But her body is sleepy. Most married women are able to identify with this, and likewise most Christians. I have taken off my robe; I am all about intimacy with you, Lord, and I love to have clean, washed feet here in our bed. But I don't want to get up; I don't want to serve anybody – just you and me, Lord. I'll get dirty in ministry. I am tired of people, tired of giving, but I love You! Let's just hide in the garden together; let's make it all about me.

The painful fact is that here is where some lovers of Christ stagnate. They follow Him into the Garden and enjoy the privacy. But there is a danger of slipping into complacency, of allowing his validation to morph into selfishness or self-preservation. Unless we hear His daily voice calling us into the newness of His mercies and the adventure of dying to self, our sinful, self-full natures will be bring decay and destitution. His life is never lifeless.

As a young believer, the difference seemed so clear between those who had drawn a line in the sand with Him and would not get out of bed, and those who were committed to following Him all the day. They related to this baby-Christian very differently. The first group consistently told me of **their** Jesus, what amazing talent He had placed in them and the grand plans He had for them. It seemed Jesus was in an impenetrable bubble with them without interest in what was outside. It left me excluded and with a taste of pride in my mouth.

The other category conveyed the same truths, but with a sense that they saw me. They were aware of who was listening to them and they intended to spark faith and encouragement in the listener. Jesus wasn't a private fan; He was eager for anyone to enjoy all that He is and offers. His love in us has open arms; it yearns to invite as He invites. It is a seed ever pushing through the soil to sprout new life and spread. In Mother Teresa's words, *It is not how much we do, but how much love we put in the doing. It is not how much we give, but how much love we put in the giving...we can do no great things; only small things with great love.*[78]

Wiersbe writes, *It is easy to fragment the Christian life and become preoccupied with individual pieces instead of the total picture. One group may emphasize "holiness" and urge its members to get victory over sin. Another may stress witnessing, or "separation from the world." But each of these emphases is really a by-product of something else: a believer's growing love for the Father. Mature Christian love is the great universal need among God's people.*[79]

"If someone says, 'I love God,' and hates his brother, he is a liar; for he who does not love his brother whom he has seen, how can he love God whom he has not seen? And this commandment we have from Him: that he who loves God must love his brother also." I John 4:20-21

There's a whopping contradiction between taking the voices of the world into the enclosed garden to sift through with Him how to respond, and then ignoring His nudge to follow Him when it's inconvenient. We are not called to follow men; they did not redeem us. However, we are to serve them as He leads. It was Solomon who wrote, "The fear of man brings a snare, but whoever trusts in the LORD shall be safe." (Proverbs 29:25) Trust in Him is an ever-deepening root. After two and a half decades in His hands, I struggle less with what were excruciating battles at first. I have tasted His sweet, sustaining comfort by my mother's casket and I live faithfully with my man. My trust in Him is now more challenged and strengthened when I face God-sized tasks in motherhood or ministry — when I am summoned to follow Him further from shore, walking on deeper waters of faith.

He remembers we are but dust (Psalm 103:14) and He is familiar with the weakness of our flesh (Matthew 26:41), but He also knows the poison of disobedience. Remember Peter's bitter tears after he had denied His Lord. (Mark 14:72) The seductive voices of self love are many and they sound so sweet to the flesh. Gautama Buddha said, *You yourself, as much as anybody in the entire universe, deserve your love and affection.* The slogan of the L'Oreal company is, **Because you're worth it**. These are distortions of the majestic, sacrificial love of the Creator into something self-imploding, shrinking, small.

Like Gollum from The Lord of the Rings, we risk becoming gradually enslaved to the dark master due to a lazy love for comfort. The very lifestyle we consider precious, applauded by an entertaining consumer culture, will corrupt us if we allow it to lull us to sleep. C.S. Lewis wrote, **Indeed the safest road to hell is the gradual one – the gentle slope, soft underfoot, without sudden turnings, without milestones, without signposts...**[80]

"Has the LORD as great delight in burnt offerings and sacrifices, as in obeying the voice of the LORD? Behold, to obey is better than sacrifice, And to heed than the fat of rams. For rebellion is as the sin of witchcraft, and stubbornness is as iniquity and idolatry. Because you have rejected the word of the LORD, He also has rejected you from being king." I Samuel 15:22b-23a

SEARCH ME, O GOD, AND KNOW MY HEART.

- *In my first, fragile steps with You, what scared me and challenged my trust?*

- *How did You steady me through it?*

- *How are You challenging my trust today?*

- *How am I responding?*

- *How am I responding when You call me into something inconvenient?*

* *As a lifestyle, do I live more in the fear of man or the fear of You?*

* *Come into my garden again, where I shield myself from Your north wind. Help me relax into Your liberating conviction. When I hesitate to follow You, Lord, forgive me and change me. Deepen my sense of Your holiness.*

Come, Fill the Gap

DAY 19

Following Him Again

Every parting gives a foretaste of death, Every reunion
a hint of the resurrection. - Arthur Schopenhauer

SONG OF SONGS 5:4-7

"My beloved put his hand by the latch of the door,
and my heart yearned for him. I arose to open for my
beloved, and my hands dripped with myrrh, my fingers
with liquid myrrh, on the handles of the lock. I opened
for my beloved, but my beloved had turned away and
was gone. My heart leaped up when he spoke. I sought
him, but I could not find him; I called him, but he
gave me no answer. The watchmen who went about the

city found me. They struck me, they wounded me; the keepers of the walls took my veil away from me."

LITERARY TREASURES

"My beloved put his hand by the latch of the door" (v. 4) beautifully reflects the invitation from Revelation 3:19-20: "As many as I love, I rebuke and chasten. Therefore be zealous and repent. Behold, I stand at the door and knock. If anyone hears My voice and opens the door, I will come in to him and dine with him, and he with Me."

The King James Version precisely translates the Hebrew "my heart yearned for Him" (v. 4) into "my bowels were moved for Him." Even this is weaker than the original, as the word for **moved** or **yearned** means **by implication to be in great commotion or tumult, to rage, war moan, clamor.**[81] Some commentaries say that He left the myrrh (v. 5) on the handle for her, reminding her of how He died for her. Remember that myrrh is a burial spice. Others read it as the bitterness of her repentance. That disagreement expresses the beauty that they mix, because they are one.

Identical to her search in chapter 3, verse 2, "I sought Him"(5:6) carries the implication of worship and prayer[82], and the **watchmen** (5:7) the protective **to hedge around.**[83] **Keepers** of the wall (5:7) is the exact same word as **watchmen.**

COME, FILL THE GAP

"My beloved put his hand by the latch of the door." (Song of Solomon 5:4) Her hesitance had closed a door between them, as reluctance so quickly does. When spending time with intelligent, warm, compassionate people who question His goodness, how quickly does their doubt seep in? So poisonous is subtle shift in perspective, as if I, we, they understand justice in this world better than He. As in Bruce Almighty, we raise our fists at how He does his God-job. When His wrath will be poured out over the earth, as described in Revelation, I almost sense God scratching His head, as He repeatedly laments, **Still they did not repent.** True to character, He intends even His wrath as an opportunity for mercy – there is still time. But there is not unlimited time. And here I am, a lover of His, at times passing judgment on His goodness, His wisdom, His ways, while I hesitate to follow.

"And my heart yearned for him. I arose to open for my beloved, and my hands dripped with myrrh, my fingers with liquid myrrh, on the handles of the lock." Song of Solomon 5:4b-5

His Spirit causes her to rise and her heart to yearn for Him, in spite of her own complacency. How I depend on His heart, pulsing through my veins, to convict and expel the poison I take in, to overcome my lethargic, lazy nature, and to throw it all off, as a dirt rag, that I might shadow Him again.

"Now He who establishes us with you in Christ and has anointed us is God, who also has sealed us and given us the Spirit in our hearts as a guarantee." 2 Corinthians 1:21-22

"I opened for my beloved, but my beloved had turned away and was gone. My heart leaped up when he spoke. I sought him, but I could not find him; I called him, but he gave me no answer." Song of Solomon 5:6

In the early days of relationship with the Lord, His presence is often almost tangible, a father next to a child on a bike newly bereft of training wheels, hovering, eager to help, catch, protect, and encourage. In those days, when she sent Him away to the Mountains of Separation, she found Him again the instant she asked her watchmen.

Not so this time. It may seem to her He is breaking their sweet intimacy, but in fact He is inviting her into a mature relationship – a partnership. As such, she must follow Him, not the reverse. In fact, He is answering her prayer, "Awake, O north wind and come, O south... Let my beloved come into His garden." (Song of Solomon 4:16) She hadn't invited His friends to come feast, but when we invites Jesus, we invite all of Him; His agenda, His friends, His sovereignty.

Like an only child with a new baby sibling, she has the choice of giving in to her jealousy or becoming part of the now expanded family as a blessing, as a helper.

Many a minister's wife struggles in a similar way. Her husband's heart is available to so many, as God has placed in Him the shepherd's heart. Ministry is not 9 to 5, and many well meaning books on marriage unintentionally isolate the spouse even further. This was my experience during the first miserable years of our marriage.

I brought to my marriage co-dependent expectations of the long, intimate eye contact I had experienced with women. My Georgia man did not meet them. He wasn't looking at me but at the crazy call God had given Him to take South Beach back from the clutches of the enemy. To me, ministry seemed like a mistress, holding his attention in a way I could not. Initially, I mourned the death of my illusion of marriage. It seemed men, after all, were the detached gender that once drove me to women.

Back in my enclosed garden, I saw my fruit withering under the heat of developing bitterness. And my Lover came, nudging me free of self-pity long enough to hear Him: *Wasn't I enough for you before you married? I am still your first Husband, and you are still to drink My living waters. His is a broken cistern. Soak your roots in Me again, and set Him free to follow Me. I will bring you together in a way you cannot.*

And as Hannah gave Samuel back to the Lord's service, so did I with my man.

"Most assuredly, I say to you, unless a grain of wheat falls into the ground and dies, it remains alone; but if it dies, it produces much grain." John 12:24

Robert and I are both free in Him, and the marriage love He has given us cannot compare to the needy infatuations of the past. At the core, I love Robert not for how he makes me feel, which is usually sweet (but not always), but for the man God is building in him. Our marriage now enjoys stronger, freer affections than human love and the call of Christ blazes in both our hearts — because His Word is powerfully true:

"But seek first the kingdom of God and His righteousness, and all these things shall be added to you." Matthew 6:33

His poetic purpose for us is, "To console those who mourn in Zion, to give them beauty for ashes, the oil of joy for mourning, the garment of praise for the spirit of heaviness; that they may be called trees of righteousness, the planting of the LORD, that He may be glorified." Isaiah 61:3

I quote this often to my women at church because its assurance is so needed in the difficult lives many of them face. He is calling us to be more than servants. He is calling us to friendship, as lovers standing eye to eye, facing each other, and as friends standing shoulder to shoulder, facing outward. We are both.

"This is My commandment, that you love one another as I have loved you. Greater love has no one than this, than to lay down one's life for his friends. You are My friends if you do whatever I command you. No longer do I call you servants, for a servant does not know what his master is doing; but I have called you friends, for all things that I heard from My Father I have made known to you. You did not choose Me, but I chose you and appointed you that you should go and bear fruit, and that your fruit should remain, that whatever you ask the Father in My name He may give you. These things I command you, that you love one another." John 15:12-17

"The watchmen who went about the city found me. They struck me, they wounded me; the keepers of the walls took my veil away from me." Song of Solomon 5:7

What!?!? I thought the watchmen were our protectors, our friends. Why did they strike her, even wound her? What does it mean that they took her veil?

The veil is her pretense, and this kind of wound often happens before great fruitfulness. Sometimes the Holy Spirit or a confrontation with someone is necessary to open our eyes to self-absorption. It is so completely against our nature to lay down our lives for someone else; we naturally prefer to give in a way that doesn't truly cost us. And there are times our pride or self-perception requires a blow; there are times the veil must be torn away, so we see as He sees. The farther we follow Him, the farther we leave our self-focus behind.

The keepers of her wall struck and wounded her, like a Shepherd at times must break the legs of a wayward lamb. She is no longer a baby; more has been given her, so more is expected. He desires truth in her inward parts.

"Obey those who rule over you, and be submissive, for they watch out for your souls, as those who must give account. Let them do so with joy and not with grief, for that would be unprofitable for you." Hebrews 13:17

"Now no chastening seems to be joyful for the present, but painful; nevertheless, afterward it yields the peaceable fruit of righteousness to those who have been trained by it. Therefore strengthen the hands which hang down, and the feeble knees, and make straight paths for your feet, so that what is lame may not be dislocated, but rather be healed." Hebrews 12:11-13

"I sought Him, but I could not find Him; I called Him, but He gave no answer." Song of Solomon 5:6b

This time He is allowing her to really comprehend the vacuum of His absence. Perhaps like Abraham with Isaac, He is testing the character of her commitment. Will she persist when the blessing of experiencing His presence is gone? What are her alternatives? What are ours, when He seems out of reach, not for a brief moment, but a painful prolonged season? Do we seek Him with more fervor, even despair – or do we turn to lesser loves?

Richard Wurmbrand spent 14 years in Romanian prisons, 3 of which were in underground isolation. He has written a gem titled, **The Triumphant Church**, on how to not only survive torture, but to do so without becoming a traitor in the process. His writings are phenomenal watchmen, stripping the western reader of illusions of grandeur. They describe the chilling reality of the majority of Christians in the world today. He saw pastors hauled in for interrogation, and many warriors for the Cross paid the ultimate price to protect their flock and stand by His Name. But there were those who collapsed under the weight, who told the persecutors the names of their brothers in Christ, and who renounced His Name. We cannot fathom the pressure of knowing our child may be taken for torture, unless we deny His Name. But we can learn from them. Those who stood firm, if they died, went straight into His Presence. If they survived, though bearing the scars and often suffering for life from the abuse, they emerged with a stronger faith and a profound awareness of His worth. But those who recanted often went insane, and many could not live with the shame and took their own lives.

What are our alternatives?

I have heard that for the finest vines, an artful caretaker will, in crucial seasons, withhold water till the plant almost dies, forcing its roots to dig deeper. Not every vine is designed for this, but those precious ones receiving this master care, bear fruits of a different caliber.

SEARCH ME, O GOD, AND KNOW MY HEART.

- *Show me, Holy Spirit, if there are areas in which I need to die.*

- *Am I following You as closely as You are calling me?*

- *Am I holding on to an image or illusion of who I am?*

- *My soul's Vinedresser, I am afraid of the process, but I still invite You to tend to me however You choose — I ask that You sustain me, so I don't wither under pressure — that my fruit be sweet to Your taste.*

Come, Fill the Gap

DAY 20
More than Any Other

A man can no more diminish God's glory by
refusing to worship Him than a lunatic can put
out the sun by scribbling the word, 'darkness'
on the walls of his cell. - C. S. Lewis[84]

SONG OF SOLOMON 5:8-16

"I charge you, O daughters of Jerusalem, if you find my beloved, that you tell him I am lovesick! What is your beloved more than another beloved, O fairest among women? What is your beloved more than another beloved, that you so charge us? My beloved is white and ruddy, Chief among ten thousand. His head is like the finest gold; His locks are wavy, and black as a raven. His eyes are like doves by the rivers of waters, washed with milk, and fitly set. His cheeks are like a bed of spices, banks of scented herbs. His lips are lilies, dripping liquid myrrh. His hands are rods of gold set with beryl. His body is carved ivory inlaid with sapphires. His legs are pillars of marble set on bases of fine gold. His countenance is like Lebanon, excellent as the cedars. His mouth is most sweet, yes, he is altogether lovely. This is my beloved, and this is my friend, O daughters of Jerusalem."

Due to the amount of verses and the cornucopia of description, today's Literary Treasures are silver threads, woven in and out of today's devotion.

COME, FILL THE GAP

"I charge you, O daughters of Jerusalem, if you find my beloved, that you tell him I am lovesick!" Song of Solomon 5:8

His absence has produced in her something close to despair, causing her to abandon the shell and draw a friend into her longing. Pretense is gone; she is not trying to play the good Christian girl. She is cut to the core and they see the true Shulamite, the authentic beloved.

How often I've seen un-saved friends of Christians, when the believer was struggling in a crisis, support that Christian's faith. Many non-Christians recognize that Jesus is what makes their friend the person they love, so they seek to strengthen the faith they see faltering.

While still dancing, very fragile in my faith, I was targeted by a new age dance teacher. *If you will go with me to these meetings, you won't believe what it will do for your dance!* I went more than once; my loyalty to my Lover was slipping. Thankfully, my father (an atheist at the time) spotted the slide, and he simply asked, *Tell me again what Jesus has done for you. Is dance worth sacrificing that?*

Tell me again what Jesus has done for you...

"What is your beloved more than another beloved, O fairest among women? What is your beloved more than another beloved, that you so charge us?" Song of Solomon 5:9

In her weakest, most depleted state, she becomes an evangelist. Her whole being is crying out for His presence, and it whets the appetite to know more.

Sometimes, the best we can do for people is to help them remember why they love someone. We are so prone to forget why we love and what He has done for us - to just remember His majesty - that He is God and we are not.

As she begins to describe Him, the spark returns to her eyes and glow of love returns to her cheeks.

Our Creator knew from the beginning that for our affections to remain His, we would need to continually remember and praise Him. So much of the Old Testament recounts the miraculous acts of the God who never failed.

"My beloved is white and ruddy, Chief among ten thousand." (Song of Solomon 5:10) *White* literally means *dazzling, sunny, bright*[85] and marvelously alludes to our Savior's glory, as seen in Revelation 1:14: "His head and hair were white like wool, as white as snow, and His eyes like a flame of fire."

The exact Hebrew word used for *ruddy* is also used, and perhaps best explained, by Isaiah 63:2: "Why is Your apparel red, And Your garments like one who treads in the winepress?" He is blazing, pure, and absolutely righteous. "He was clothed with a robe dipped in blood, and His name is called The Word of God. And the armies in heaven, clothed in fine linen, white and clean, followed Him on white horses." Revelation 19:13-14

Chief literally means "*standard bearer, that is, as conspicuous above all others, as a standard bearer is among hosts. The chief of sinners needs the 'chiefest' of Saviors.*[86]

Will we embrace the apparent contradictions? His blazing holiness and red-hot righteousness meet in His own blood. And it was exactly for our disobedience He died. His purity sanctifies. Refuge is on offer under His banner of love. He, to whom we have entrusted our lives and hearts, is pure goodness. He has all authority, and He is for us.

"His head is like the finest gold; His locks are wavy and black as a raven". (5:11) When Moses anointed Aaron as the first earthly high priest, "he put the turban on his head. Also on the turban, on its front, he put the golden plate, the holy crown, as the LORD had commanded Moses." (Leviticus 8:9) A universal symbol of kingship is a golden crown. Our Beloved is both our High Priest, ever interceding for us, and the highest King in the universe. All others receive authority from Him.

John Gill suggests that His wavy locks are symbolic of His countless believers, as "Children's children are the crown of old men, and the glory of children is their father." (Proverbs 17:6) In heaven, His hair is brighter than white, but here among us, *his locks are said to be black, to set forth his juvenile vigor and strength, which is always in its bloom, without any change or alteration: He is the mighty God in his highest nature, and 'mighty to save' as mediator; he gave the fullest proof of his strength and courage in fulfilling all the law required, in bearing all that justice inflicted, and in conquering all His and our enemies.*[87]

Perhaps the flames that burn away impurities and fortify faith bring crowns as rewards. Certainly, perseverance in faith brings joy and even a crown to those who have prayed for us. Who is that in your life? Who has carried you before His throne in intercession and love? Think of them when you are tempted to give up, to hesitate, to retreat from the fire back to unbelief. "For what is our hope, or joy, or crown of rejoicing? Is it not even you in the presence of our Lord Jesus Christ at His coming? For you are our glory and joy." I Thessalonians 2:19-20

He knows every stomach cramp and every sleepless hour - perhaps these very flames will bring such fine gold that soon, you will place this crown at his wounded feet, when you see him face to face.

"His eyes are like doves by the rivers of waters, washed with milk, and fitly set." Song of Solomon 5:12

The innocence and lifelong faithfulness He beholds in your eyes are reflections of Himself. When His Father proclaimed him, "My beloved Son, in whom I am well pleased" (Matthew 3:17), the heavens were opened and the Spirit of God descended like a dove. Perhaps these rivers of water refer to His baptism, when He indentified so completely with us that He could bear our suffering.

When we look into another's eyes, it is a mirror. And the River of Life flows through His eyes, as the milk of His Word washes. His eyes are fitly set, as a gem in a ring, - as the precious stones in the high priest's breast plate. Because He experienced the brutality of this earth, there is profound compassion and mercy, as He ever intercedes for us.

"His cheeks are like a bed of spices, banks of scented herbs. His lips are lilies, dripping liquid myrrh." Song of Solomon 5:13

The cheeks were considered a seat of beauty, yet we smote and spat on them and pulled His beard out. It is precisely this humiliation and sacrifice that make them now like a raised garden bed of fragrant healing ointment. By His wounds we are healed and there is balsam in His cheeks. His lips are soft, gentle, and pure like lilies, dripping His sacrifice, His principles of life and death and resurrection.

"You are fairer than the sons of men; grace is poured upon Your lips; therefore God has blessed You forever." Psalm 45:2

"His hands are rods of gold set with beryl. His body is carved ivory inlaid with sapphires." Song of Solomon 5:14

His hands, driven through with rusty nails, so they could hold you forever, are now gold. They are made of the stuff of Heaven, where mansions await. His body, His bowels, His seat of compassion are likewise pure, sky blue, as a horizon where heaven and earth kiss, boundless and strong as eternity.

"His legs are pillars of marble set on bases of fine gold. His countenance is like Lebanon, excellent as the cedars." Song of Solomon 5:15

His legs are pillars of strength and steadfastness. Though the neighboring thieves' legs were broken on their crosses, His were not. His life and death tried Him as through fire, and He is purified gold. His countenance, the face of undivided attention and affection, evokes the cedars of Lebanon, enduring and providing shelter.

"The LORD also will roar from Zion, and utter His voice from Jerusalem; the heavens and earth will shake; but the LORD will be a shelter for His people, and the strength of the children of Israel." Joel 3:16

"His mouth is most sweet, yes, he is altogether lovely. This is my beloved, and this is my friend, O daughters of Jerusalem!" Song of Solomon 5:16

His mouth, His Word, His kiss - is most sweet! Oh, that we could fathom His sweetness, His majesty, His holiness, His altogether love-liness! Oh, that we could fathom His stronger-than-the-universe love for us!

Help us, Holy Spirit....

"And when He had said this, He breathed on them, and said to them, 'Receive the Holy Spirit.'" John 20:22

"Then I turned to see the voice that spoke with me. And having turned I saw seven golden lamp stands, and in the midst of the seven lamp stands One like the Son of Man, clothed with a garment down to the feet and girded about the chest with a golden band. His head and hair were white like wool, as white as snow, and His eyes like a flame of fire; His feet were like fine brass, as if refined in a furnace, and His voice as the sound of many waters; He had in His right hand seven stars, out of His mouth went a sharp two-edged sword, and His countenance was like the sun shining in its strength." Revelation 1:12-16

SEARCH ME, O GOD, AND KNOW MY HEART!

- *Open my eyes to Your majesty, Your sweetness, and Your devotion. Spirit of the Living God, fall afresh on me.*

- *How do I lift you up among my friends? How would they say I describe You?*

- *As I journey through the fire, let me know you are with me.*

- *King of Kings, today I afresh commit these aspects of my life under Your authority:*

- *Living Word, open my eyes to see You in Your majesty. Let these praises of mine be jewels in Your crown.*

DAY 21

Awesome as an Army with Banners

There are a hundred men hacking at the branches of evil to every one who is striking at the roots of evil. - Henry Ward Beecher[88]

SONG OF SOLOMON 6:1-5A

"Where has your beloved gone, O fairest among women? Where has your beloved turned aside, that we may seek him with you? My beloved has gone to his garden, to the beds of spices, to feed in the gardens, and to gather lilies. I am my beloved's, and my beloved is mine. He feeds his flock among the lilies. O my love, you are as beautiful as Tirzah, lovely *as Jerusalem, awesome as an army with banners! Turn your eyes away from me, for they have overcome me."*

LITERARY TREASURES

Seamlessly, the three voices of our song blend into harmony. The daughters of Jerusalem pose the question that will unite them. *O fairest among women* (6:1) is verbatim the sweet phrase He used in chapter 1, verse 8 when asked where He would feed His flock. In hearing it, she immediately remembers where he is, "My beloved has gone…to feed in the gardens." (6:2) The moment she remembers, His voice of assurance returns, "O My love…" Song of Solomon 6:4

The implication of the Hebrew verb translated **to feed** (6:2) is **to tend a flock, that is to pasture it.**[89] He never abdicates His shepherding role, even as He disciplines. "If you endure chastening, God deals with you as with sons; for what son is there whom a father does not chasten?" (Hebrews 12:7) "I am the good shepherd. The good shepherd gives His life for the sheep." John 10:11

"Beautiful as Tirzah, lovely as Jerusalem." (6:4) *Tirzah* signifies pleasant, well-pleasing, and was at this time the capital of the north (Israel), as Jerusalem was of the south (Judah). Jerusalem contains the word **shalom** as a hidden treasure, as does Solomon and Shulamite.

COME, FILL THE GAP

After her breathtaking description of this majestic, death-conquering, infinitely compassionate Lover, the yearning of her friends has awakened to the point of action:

"Where has your beloved gone, O fairest among women? Where has your beloved turned aside, that we may seek Him with you?" Song of Solomon 6:1

From her state of exasperated yearning, she had reached into her reservoir of knowledge of Him, and what came out was raw and true. When Jesus is lifted up in our speech and focus, in the direction of our heart, He draws people unto Himself. Our religious activities, our own righteousness, our political views, whatever other purposes they serve, do not tend to draw people to Jesus.

"And I, if I am lifted up from the earth, will draw all peoples to Myself." John 12:32

"And as Moses lifted up the serpent in the wilderness, even so must the Son of Man be lifted up." (John 3:14) Jesus was reminding His listener, a fearful, but awakening Pharisee, of Israel's history. In the wilderness, God's own people, whom He just delivered from centuries of brutal slavery, spoke out against God and Moses. They accused them, like we sometimes do during a natural disaster. We slither into the pride that we are more compassionate and just than God. Suffering is fathomless and impenetrable. **Why does God allow it?** These men, women, and children in the desert were very hungry and thirsty. No food or water in sight. Why?

Later we read that God tested them there; apparently He expected trust, even then. Apparently, He expected remembrance of miracles He had already performed. He brings us to places of drought and hunger and then desires us to invite Him to fill those gaps. The Bread of Life, the Living Water, somehow He expects us to rely on His sufficiency.

"And the people spoke against God and against Moses: 'Why have you brought us up out of Egypt to die in the wilderness? For there is no food and no water, and our soul loathes this worthless bread.'

So the LORD sent fiery serpents among the people, and they bit the people; and many died. Therefore the people came to Moses, and said, 'We have sinned, for we have spoken against the LORD and against you; pray to the LORD that He take away the serpents from us.' So Moses prayed for the people. Then the LORD said to Moses, 'Make a fiery serpent, and set it on a pole; and it shall be that everyone who is bitten, when he looks at it, shall live.' So Moses made a bronze serpent, and put it on a pole; and so it was, if a serpent had bitten anyone, when he looked at the bronze serpent, he lived." Numbers 21:5-9

This is the passage Jesus refers back to, right before the famous **For God so loved the world** Scripture. He would be lifted up on the Cross, as that fiery serpent was set on a pole.

A serpent in the Garden of Eden led to the curse, under which the whole earth groans. The staff in Aaron's hand became a serpent before Pharaoh. Fiery serpents were the consequence of the whining unbelief of the Israelites — and the healing remedy would be a bronze serpent. Looking at it would bring life.

Thus must the Son of Man be lifted up!

Song of Solomon specifically speaks the language of romantic longing. Nothing causes the groans of hunger and thirst — to speak against God in thought or deed - as much as romantic longings misdirected. Aching, insatiable, my parched soul condemned Him:

Why did You make me a lesbian and then forbid I love women? Why did you give me a man who doesn't even see me? "My soul loathes this worthless bread." Numbers 21:5

He didn't send me fiery serpents; He sent me a passionate Savior. I looked into His lavishly loving eyes, and in His acceptance I saw my own shallow, muddy desires for what they were. I saw that my impure, lesser loves caused Him to, of His free will, be lifted up like a serpent on a pole in the wilderness.

"For God so loved the world that He gave His only begotten Son, that whoever believes in Him should not perish but have everlasting life. For God did not send His Son into the world to condemn the world, but that the world through Him might be saved." John 3:16-17

Not only did He save me, but He so thoroughly redeemed my love for women, that in the same place I once thirsted for affection and tenderness, He allows me to pour out His affections and tenderness.

"I say to you that likewise there will be more joy in heaven over one sinner who repents than over ninety-nine just persons who need no repentance." Luke 15:7

As the Shulamite, whose name reflects Solomon, remembers who He is and realizes the need of her friends to find Him, she suddenly knows exactly where He is. He is in His garden, of course, feeding His flock among the lilies. That's who He is. That's what He does. And for the first time, she embraces that being her Beloved's means feeding His flock with Him.

When Peter denies his relationship with Jesus three times, Jesus asks three times, **Do you love Me?**

For each failure, He gives us a chance to affirm our love – and each time, it is interwined with feeding His flock.

"So when they had eaten breakfast, Jesus said to Simon Peter, 'Simon, son of Jonah, do you love Me more than these?' He said to Him, 'Yes, Lord; You know that I love You.' He said to him, 'Feed My lambs.' He said to him again a second time, 'Simon, son of Jonah, do you love Me?' He said to Him, 'Yes, Lord; You know that I love You.' He said to him, 'Tend My sheep.' He said to him the third time,

'Simon, son of Jonah, do you love Me?' Peter was grieved because He said to him the third time, 'Do you love Me?' And he said to Him, 'Lord, You know all things; You know that I love You.' Jesus said to him, 'Feed My sheep. Most assuredly, I say to you, when you were younger, you girded yourself and walked where you wished; but when you are old, you will stretch out your hands, and another will gird you and carry you where you do not wish.' This He spoke, signifying by what death he would glorify God. And when He had spoken this, He said to him, 'Follow Me'. John 21:15-19

"O My love, you are as beautiful as Tirzah, lovely as Jerusalem, awesome as an army with banners!" Song of Solomon 6:4

Pleasant, well-pleasing Tirzah, capital of the north, exemplified loveliness, security, and loyalty. Jerusalem, capital the south, was called city of peace. His praise stretches both north and south; it includes both kingdoms; it is a resonance of His longing for our unity.

"There is neither Jew nor Greek, there is neither slave nor free, there is neither male nor female; for you are all one in Christ Jesus." Galatians 3:28

Favoritism and disdain in the church grieves His Spirit. When reading **Uncle Tom's Cabin**[90], I was completely baffled by the attempts to justify slavery scripturally, and I've asked my American husband how people who came here as pilgrims could create the Trail of Tears. Trust me, I am no ungrateful foreigner passing judgment on the nation that has so hospitably welcomed me. This is not unique to any civilization. In **When a Nation Forgets God, 7 Lessons we Must Learn from Nazi Germany**[91], Erwin W. Lutzer grapples with the subtle choices in the German church that gradually diluted it, until it became just another arm of Hitler's choke-hold. Shamefully, one church member recalls singing hymns while hearing the screams of the Jews in the boxcars on the railroad next to the church. With

Nazi precision, the doomed cargo would always pass by during the service. Lutzer documents,

We became disturbed when we heard the cries coming from the train as it passed by. We realized that it was carrying Jews like cattle in the cars! ... Their screams tormented us. We knew the time the train was coming and when we heard the whistle blow we began singing hymns. By the time the train came past our church we were singing at the top of our voices. If we heard the screams, we sang more loudly and soon we heard them no more. Years have passed and no one talks about it anymore. But I still hear that train whistle in my sleep. God forgive me; forgive all of us who called ourselves Christians yet did nothing to intervene.

Should Jesus delay His return, I wonder what future generations will find cruel and bizarre about us, wondering how we tolerated it. Come, open our eyes! May we be beautiful as Tirzah, lovely as Jerusalem!

"Awesome as an army with banners!" Song of Solomon 6:4

She has proclaimed Him **Chief among ten thousand.** (Song of Solomon 5:10) He is the Chief, and we are the army. The word **awesome** literally means **terrible, awe-inspiring.**[92]

What would you fight for? When I survey the realities of slavery, the Trail of Tears, the Nazi horrors, I want to be awesome as an army with banners. When I watch the famine and civil war in Somalia, when I hear of the millions of young girls who willfully kill or are deceived into aborting their babies, when I think of the sex slavery right here in the strip clubs we pass daily, when _____(you fill in the blank), I want to be awesome as an army with banners.

I wish to open the eyes of loved ones unable to see His majesty. I wish to articulate how the social justice, they long for, is found in Him, their scientific objections dwarfed and disproved. I wish to sing the song of Heaven so that they might hear. I would give anything!

So I follow the Chief among ten thousand. Yes, He can!

What arouses the warrior princess within you?

This description **awesome as an army with banners** is so significant to Him that He repeats it a few verses later (6:10). Your Word is true – arouse us!

"May He grant you according to your heart's desire, and fulfill all your purpose. We will rejoice in your salvation, and in the name of our God we will set up our banners! May the LORD fulfill all your petitions." Psalm 20:4-5

Watching her adopt His Lover-Warrior identity, He exclaims, "Turn your eyes away from Me, for they have overcome Me." (Song of Solomon 6:5) Literally, they have taken Me by storm! Your oneness with My flock and your fire to fight for My flock under My banner of love – they take Me by storm!

He is more passionate than we – more able to be ravished – He is more!

Don't ever think your appetite too big, your vision too ambitious, or your taste buds too well-developed. C.S. Lewis mused,

It would seem that Our Lord finds our desires not too strong, but too weak. We are half-hearted creatures, fooling about with drink and sex and ambition when infinite joy is offered us, like an ignorant child who wants to go on making mud pies in a slum because he cannot imagine what is

meant by the offer of a holiday at the sea. We are far too easily pleased.[93]

The grandest display of beauty in the human imagination is a weak, colorless, depleted version of what He created before the curse corrupted and twisted His original. The strongest infatuation we know is handicapped by the sheer smallness of our emotions. We have no conception of the extent to which selfishness is our warped, natural filter.

But His love is stronger and it frees us and re-creates us and gives us His air to breathe. His love is pure; it never seeks its own. Praising Him, focusing on His majesty is the reality check; it brings much needed perspective. C.S. Lewis also said, **You and I have need of the strongest spell that can be found to wake us from the evil enchantment of worldliness.**[94]

"For the LORD takes pleasure in His people; He will beautify the humble with salvation. Let the saints be joyful in glory; let them sing aloud on their beds. Let the high praises of God be in their mouth, and a two-edged sword in their hand." Psalm 149:4-6

SEARCH ME, O GOD, AND KNOW MY HEART.

- *Is there a specific failure in my life, where You long to show me specific redemption?*

- *In what way can I bring unity in my world?*

- *Where does Your battle cry inside me lead? Which battle is mine?*

- *Oh, Chief among ten thousand, let me recognize Your battle cry inside and show me how to be the hands and feet of Your love. I will follow you all the way.*

DAY 22
My Only One

*There is not an inch of any sphere of life
of which Jesus Christ the Lord does not
say, 'Mine.' - Abraham Kuyper[95]*

SONG OF SOLOMON 6:5-10

"Turn your eyes away from me, for they have overcome me. Your hair is like a flock of goats going down from Gilead. Your teeth are like a flock of sheep which have come up from the washing; every one bears twins, and none is barren among them. Like a piece of pome- granate are your temples behind your veil. There are sixty queens and eighty concubines, and virgins without number. My dove, my perfect one, is the only one, the only one of her mother, the favorite of the one who bore her. The daughters saw her and called her blessed, the queens and the concubines, and they praised her. Who is she who looks forth as the morning, fair as the moon, clear as the sun, Awesome as an army with banners?"

LITERARY TREASURES

"Hair like a flock of goats"…"teeth like a flock of sheep"…"like a piece of pomegranate are your temples" (Song of Solomon 6:6-7) are word for word the same praises He lavished on her in chapter 4. Jamieson, Faucett, and Brown suggest that *sixty* means an indefinite number, as with the valiant warriors in 3:7.

At this point, their internal language, as hopefully ours, has been established. When God repeats himself in the Word, it is for emphasis and perhaps because we are so prone to forget the truth and the power it contains. Thus **My dove** again refers to the enduring faithfulness of His Holy Spirit within us and **her mother** to the church. Notice yet another echo of her earlier words, as He turns around her question from chapter 3, verse 6 and asks "Who is she?" (Song of Solomon 6:10)

COME, FILL THE GAP

When I first met my man, I had an instant sense of recognition, as if I already knew him. But there was no chance of that; I had just arrived on a plane from Copenhagen; these were my first days in the States. Then he taught my class in Youth With A Mission, and again that sense that I knew him; I recognized something I couldn't define, like a fragrance transporting me back to some place I couldn't quite put my finger on.

For the first and only time in my life, I fell head over heels in love with a man, and it completely blindsided me. I didn't even recognize what was happening, a child too young, tasting wine and feeling its effects. Woozy! Suddenly, nothing else existed, no coherent thoughts were present; and the man I so admired and **recognized**, I barely knew. Somehow, I saw the man he was becoming. But as the agony of our clueless, early marriage testifies, he wasn't all that yet. Nor was I whatever it was he saw in me. We saw in each other what we were becoming; we saw seeds that had yet to die and be transformed.

Jesus, with perfect vision, sees the seeds and speaks life. When He first declared her attributes in chapter 4, she wasn't there yet. Her heart wasn't ready to follow Him, and He knew. So He spoke a transformed identity to her, to the seed inside her, then He sifted her, by allowing the watchmen to wound. "Faithful are the wounds of a friend." (Proverbs 27:6) He tore off her illusions. Her sincerity deepened as she tasted His absence, and now He speaks it over her again.

"There are sixty queens and eighty concubines, and virgins without number. My dove, my perfect one, is the only one, the only one of her mother, the favorite of the one who bore her. The daughters saw her and called her blessed, the queens and the concubines, and they praised her." Song of Solomon 6:8-9

Solomon would know! These numbers are fractions of his actual queens and concubines, all of them in violation of God's expressed will. This is yet another example of culture accepting as normal what God does not. The most sacred union on earth, marriage, matters profoundly to our Groom, as it is intended to express His heart to His Bride.

"Therefore a man shall leave his father and mother and be joined to his wife and the two shall become one flesh." Genesis 2:24

Jesus left heaven behind to become one with us.

"Then I will give them one heart, and I will put a new spirit within them, and take the stony heart out of their flesh, and give them a heart of flesh, that they may walk in My statutes and keep My judgments and do them; and they shall be My people, and I will be their God." Ezekiel 11:19-20

There are sixty celebrities and eighty powerful politicians and great people without number. But My dove, My perfect one, is the only one. My daughter and I sometimes discuss whether this or that singer may be Christian. **But they are so good! They almost sing about Jesus**, she pleads. You may have someone in mind, whom you wish were redeemed, so you could give yourself more to their influence. My very first prayer as a newborn Christian was for my favorite singer – I couldn't bear the thought of Heaven without her music.

On the flipside, you may have something to offer, and the **enchantment of worldliness** may be tugging at your convictions, a compromise under the guise that once you have the coveted position, you will be a light for Jesus. In the glamour of South Beach, many a virgin became a concubine under that spell.

When the mother of Zebedee's sons asked of Jesus that her sons would sit on either side of Him in Heaven, Jesus answered, "You do not know what you are asking. Can you drink the cup that I am going to drink?" (Matthew 20:22) The cup of dying to self is in opposition to the cup self-promotion. Often, both the faith and the career are ship-wrecked. These sons assured Him that they could indeed drink the cup – and they did – but even then He couldn't guarantee their coveted positions. "These are not mine to grant; they belong to those to whom they have been allotted by My Father." Matthew 20:23

What will position give us, make us, do for us? Why is it so important even among believers, to grasp for recognition that we've turned His house of prayer into a marketplace? Are we indistinguishable from the world in vying for man's approval? Don't we know that it wars directly against our faith: "How can you believe, who receive honor from one another, and do not seek the honor that comes from the only God?" John 5:44

None are immune — but recognize that significance from man is water from a broken cistern. It is an insult to Him. Like the Israelites in the desert, our worldly strivings are loudly announcing to anyone watching that He is not sufficient! We need others to fill our gaps. Like you, I am a fellow, hungry sojourner, hoping we recognize that the flirt with human idolatry is not our friend; it does not have our best interest at heart; it wars against faith.

"My dove, my perfect one, is the only one, the only one of her mother, the favorite of the one who bore her. The daughters saw her and called her blessed, the queens and the concubines, and they praised her." Song of Solomon 6:9

Ever seen a little girl who just discovered she is cute? When she tries to milk it, to fabricate the charm, it evaporates. But a child still unaware, who is doing what comes natural, is adorable. Much in the same way, when we are not milking it, striving for it, praise and affirmation find us. And much more deeply satisfying, when living life in His light, those around us recognize His blessing. It's beautiful and visible when uncorrupted.

His well of Living water never runs dry; with Him our needs can be boundless, and He loves us more. Dip your sponge for significance and validation in that healing, life-giving River.

"There is a river whose streams shall make glad the city of God, God is in the midst of her; she shall not be moved; God shall help her, just at the break of dawn. The holy place of the tabernacle of the Most High." Psalm 46:4-5

"Who is she who looks forth as the morning, fair as the moon, clear as the sun, awesome as an army with banners?" Song of Solomon 6:10

You are *just at the break of dawn, looking forth as the morning*. Look forward! Don't be pulled back by yesterday's mistakes; His mercies are new every morning. I threw out today's paper – I'll get a new one tomorrow, a current one. Let His streams make glad and new; let the old depart. He, who is eternal, will preserve that in you which has eternal value. Let go of what doesn't. Look to the Morning star and reflect Him. The moon shines in a dark world, testifying that the Sun still shines. By looking forward and looking upward, you reflect Him – awesome as an army with banners - ever more coming alive.

SEARCH ME, O GOD, AND KNOW MY HEART.

* *Where do I look for significance?*

* *Am I in any way 'under the evil enchantment of worldliness'?*

- *Do I look forward and upward, or more inward and backwards?*

- *O Lord, as much as I know how, I commit my hopes and dreams to You alone. I want you to be my Only One, and I invite You to fill all of me.*

Come, Fill the Gap

DAY 23

Chariot of My People

*I have but one candle of life to burn, and I would
rather burn it out in a land filled with darkness than
in a land flooded with light. - John Keith Falconer[96]*

SONG OF SOLOMON 6:11-7:1

"I went down to the garden of nuts to see the ver-
dure of the valley, to see whether the vine had budded and the pomegranates had bloomed. Before I was
even aware, my soul had made me as the chariots of my
noble people. Return, return, O Shulamite; return,
return, that we may look upon you! What would you
see in the Shulamite - as it were, the dance of the
two camps? How beautiful are your feet in sandals,

O prince's daughter! The curves of your thighs are like jewels, the work of the hands of a skillful workman."

LITERARY TREASURES

Again, the melodious blend of the three voices of the beloved believer (6:11-12), her friends (6:13), and the Lover of her soul (7:1) appear.

You might imagine how my ladies laughed when I first mentioned *the garden of nuts*. (Song of Solomon 6:11) We looked at each other and very much felt it described us! But though we are a peculiar people, there is rich symbolism here. **The walnut is composed of a bitter outer husk, a hard shell, and sweet kernel. Likewise, the Word is distasteful to the careless; when awakened, the sinner finds the letter hard, until the Holy Ghost reveals the sweet inner spirit.**[97]

The coherency of God's Word is breathtaking. Do you hear **whether the wine had budded** alluding to the words of Jesus in John 15:5? "I am the vine, you are the branches. He who abides in Me, and I in him, bears much fruit; for without Me you can do nothing."

COME, FILL THE GAP

This time she comes as His desired co-gardener, helping Him tend the garden, to gauge the maturity of the fruits there. Fruits plucked too early are either sour or bitter — or they ripen away from their tree into blandness, like most of the exotic fruits in the super-mart. A wise Gardner, not pressured by production goals, allows the time necessary for the maturation process.

A pastor of a church faces great difficulty in this regard. As Christians, we often think we are further along the path of spiritual growth than we really are; and as mentioned, we sometimes convert a role in ministry into a source of significance. Immaturity, combined with a need to be important, is a toxic mix. A wise pastor foresees the agony that follows too much responsibility too soon and protects everyone involved by not 'plucking that fruit' yet. How much sweeter and juicier, how much more nourishment is found when we, like He, take the time to inspect and to wait for enough sun, rain, snow or drought to complete the growing, as He designed it!

"Before I was even aware, My soul had made me as the chariots of my noble people." Song of Solomon 6:12

Forgetting herself by His side in the garden, she became **a chariot for her noble people**. In chapter 1, He compared to her a filly among Pharaoh's chariots. At the time, she was young, being trained for her royal responsibility. Now, while not even pursuing it, she became one who carries her people.

"Then it happened, as they continued on and talked, that suddenly a chariot of fire appeared with horses of fire, and separated the two of them; and Elijah went up by a whirlwind into heaven." 2 Kings 2:11

I long to be such a chariot, carrying noble people into heaven. As the birth pains intensify, I am increasingly alarmed by loved ones who may not be ready when He arrives to whirl us out of this brief existence.

"Return, return, O Shulamite; return, return, that we may look upon you! What would you see in the Shulamite - as it were, the dance of the two camps?" Song of Solomon 6:13

If I could tell you what it meant, there would be no point in dancing it, thought Isadora Duncan, ever on a quest to find truth in dance. I doubt she found His truth, but her words express how I feel about this Song; I wish I could dance it for you – I long to see Him dance it for us.

We see the beloved primed as a chariot for her people; she becomes one who escorts her people to heaven, the chariot that fetched Home Elijah.

Now her friends are intrigued and calling her back; they want to see what is happening to her. They recognize Him shining through her and call her Shulamite. They call her by the feminine version of Solomon; they perceive the Prince of Peace in her, and they want to gaze at her to behold that which they barely understand but to which they are drawn. She is no longer merely one of them; she is dancing between two camps.

When I first landed on American soil, I was a complete foreigner. I may have left my country behind, but it was Danish attitudes, tastes, and accent that defined me. When I first went back, I was coming home. But somewhere the internal attachment shifted, and I gradually became a visitor in a country that had moved on without me. It was disconcerting; I felt rootless. Then came a season where I so identified with America that I lost appreciation for the place I once called home. It's been twenty years now, and though my clear allegiance is to the United States (upon becoming a naturalized citizen I even had to swear to take up arms) I savor my heritage, and sometimes venture into IKEA for a whiff of childhood.

The dance of the two camps is different for each of us. Some cling to the old country, old friends, habits, and places, after becoming citizens of Heaven. There is nostalgia and often a caution to seem disrespectful to friends who have been loyal and whose support is still there. We tip-toe between the two camps. For these new citizens, forming bonds in church is often easier said than done, because we do relate differently and new friendships don't initially compare with lifelong friendships. My hand was so full of my own choices that there was very little space left for God.

Then there are those, like my man, who are so radically changed, so powerfully jolted alive by His Spirit – that everybody around them is affected. This is often where evangelism happens, because the enthusiasm is so fresh and the relationships with old friends are intact. People around them either love them or hate them because these converts are not so much dancing as stomping between the two camps.

How would He have us dance between the camp of the people we came out of and the peculiar people we are adopted into?

The poetic schizophrenia from chapter 1, "I am dark, but lovely" (Song of Solomon 1:5) sings about identity and alludes to how Jesus and His intercessors identify with the two camps. I wish I could dance these truths, rather than grasping for words to express them. I long to see you dance them in your new body when we enjoy His presence together in His throne room. I long for us to dance with Him together.

In Paul's blinding first encounter with the Lord, he heard a Voice asking, "Saul, Saul, why are you persecuting Me?" (Acts 9:4) Jesus expresses that He is One with the church. When Isaiah saw the Lord on His glorious throne with the smoke of our prayers and the seraphim proclaiming that the whole earth was full of His glory, his first response was, "Woe is me, for I am undone! Because I am a man of unclean lips, and I dwell in the midst of a people of unclean lips; for my eyes have seen the King, The LORD of hosts." Isaiah 6:5

I am dark, but lovely. I am redeemed, but I still have the same propensity to sin as do the people I live among. I'm not suddenly above my unsaved peers, but I am His. His coal has touched my lips, not only so I praise Him, but so I tell the people - so I develop into their chariot. Like Isaiah, the more we see His glory and holiness, the more we fear for those untouched by His coal.

"Then one of the seraphim flew to me, having in his hand a live coal which he had taken with the tongs from the altar. And he touched my mouth with it, and said: 'Behold, this has touched your lips; your iniquity is taken away, and your sin purged.' Also I heard the voice of the Lord, saying: 'Whom shall I send, and who will go for Us?' Then I said, 'Here am I! Send me.' And He said, 'Go, and tell this people'. Isaiah 6:6-9

About his book *Erasing Hell*[98], Francis Chan urges, *I have to warn people. I don't want people going [to hell]. And if they ignore it, there's a much more likely chance that they'll end up there. Obviously, I don't take light the sovereignty of God, but looking at it from a pragmatic perspective, it's like canoeing before the Niagara Falls. If you don't know it's there or you've got deceived that it's not there there's no drop off.*

"How beautiful are your feet in sandals, O prince's daughter! The curves of your thighs are like jewels, the work of the hands of a skillful workman." Song of Solomon 7:1

Your feet literally means *your goings*. How beautiful are your goings in sandals, not combat boots that could hurt those to whom you're sent, not bare feet, unprotected and vulnerable. We dance well in sandals, and He will protect our goings between these camps, He will enlarge the path beneath us, so our feet don't slip, and He, who is like a gazelle, will enable us to leap over walls to reach those we love. Psalm 18

Until the industrializing era, family businesses were inherited, and the typical global lifestyle was for mother, father, and children to work side by side in a trade they had honed for generations. As children of God and joint heirs with Jesus Christ, our common family endeavor is "preaching good tidings to the poor, healing the brokenhearted, proclaiming liberty to the captives, comforting all who mourn, giving them beauty for ashes, the oil of joy for mourning, The garment of praise for the spirit of heaviness; That they may be called trees of righteousness, The planting of the LORD, that He may be glorified." Isaiah 61:1-3

We embrace this calling by prioritizing family unity:

"That they all may be one, as You, Father, are in Me, and I in You; that they also may be one in Us, that the world may believe that You sent Me. And the glory which You gave Me I have given them, that they may be one just as We are one: I in them, and You in Me; that they may be made perfect in one, and that the world may know that You have sent Me, and have loved them as You have loved Me." John 17:21-23

We embrace this calling by allowing His love to radiate through us: *Her glories are her Lord's, beaming through her. The two armies are the family of Jesus Christ in heaven, and that on earth, joined and one with Him; the one militant, the other triumphant. Or Jesus Christ and His ministering angels are one army, the Church the other, both being one. Though she is peace, yet she has warfare here, between flesh and spirit within and foes without; her strength is Jesus Christ and His host enlisted on her side by prayer; whence she obtains those graces which raise the admiration of the daughters of Jerusalem.*[99]

We embrace this calling and by going where He sends us:

"How beautiful upon the mountains are the feet of him who brings good news, who proclaims peace, who brings glad tidings of good things, who proclaims salvation, who says to Zion, 'Your God reigns!'" Isaiah 52:7

You are the prince's daughter as much as His sister and beloved. As He sends you like a dove among wolves, His Father's heart is ever watching to enlarge your path. His love is so all-encompassing that every human relationship you have is carefully monitored by the fiercely protective eye of a father on his only young daughter.

SEARCH ME, O GOD, AND KNOW MY HEART.

- *Make me Your chariot and selfless laborer in Your vineyard whose face is towards You, looking for Your return. Have a rich harvest among those I love...*

- *How well do I dance between the two camps?*

- *To whom specifically are You sending me to proclaim peace?*

- *Am I in any way dancing too close to the edge?*

- *My Maker, let me hear You whisper my name, as You send me on the family mission. Give me Your heart for my old camp and all the courage from Your camp. Touch my lips! Here I am.*

DAY 24 : CHARIOT OF MY PEOPLE

DAY 24

Communion

*Like when you sit in front of a fire in winter - You are
just there in front of the fire. You don't have to be smart
or anything. The fire warms you.* - Desmond Tutu

SONG OF SOLOMON 7:2

*"Your navel is a rounded goblet; it lacks
no blended beverage. Your waist is a heap
of wheat set about with lilies."*

As the Song of Solomon is a poetic potpourri of the divine romance
expressed throughout the Bible, so in this mysterious little verse we
find the same in its most concentrated form.

LITERARY TREASURES

Navel literally means *umbilical chord.*[100] *Blended beverage* comes from a root verb meaning *to mingle water and wine.*[101] I will refer to the *rounded goblet* as a chalice or a communion cup. *Your waist* contains the implication of *womb*[102].

For *wheat* and *lilies*, we look to Scripture to interpret Scripture. Jesus refers to Himself as "the bread of life" (John 6:36) and teaches the most characteristic life principle of His followers: "Most assuredly, I say to you, unless a grain of wheat falls into the ground and dies, it remains alone; but if it dies, it produces much grain. He who loves his life will lose it, and he who hates his life in this world will keep it for eternal life. If anyone serves Me, let him follow Me; and where I am, there My servant will be also. If anyone serves Me, him My Father will honor." John 12:24-26

About the *lilies*, He said in chapter 2, verse 2 "Like a lily among thorns, so is my love among the daughters." And in the words of Jesus, "Consider the lilies, how they grow: they neither toil nor spin; and yet I say to you, even Solomon in all his glory was not arrayed like one of these." Luke 12:27

COME, FILL THE GAP

Your umbilical chord is like a communion cup; it lacks no water and wine mixed. *The symbols of blood and wine were connected in biblical times. The Jews recognized blood as a life force, created injunctions against consuming it, shed it as a sin offering, fearing being defiled by it, and recalled it as a sign of the covenant with God in their annual celebration of deliverance at Passover.*[103] And it is the ultimate sign of His covenant with you.

"'Come now, and let us reason together,' says the LORD, 'Though your sins are like scarlet, they shall be as white as snow; though they are red like crimson, they shall be as wool.'" Isaiah 1:18

The most fundamental life source is His broken heart (blood and water in John 19:34), His innocent blood poured out, so that every wrong ever done is covered. His heart broke when His Father had to turn His face away from Him, as all the monstrous sin of the ages was heaped on Him. We were crucified with Him that day, and when He defeated death, it was with us in mind. His blood now flows in our veins.

It is the life of Christ and our life blended together into one life. As we drink the cup, we drink the cup that Jesus drank, but we also drink our cup. That is the great mystery of the Eucharist.[104] When the sons of Zebedee were grasping for position, Jesus asked if they could drink the cup. (Matthew 20:20-23) Embrace the life He has for you with the deaths and resurrections it entails. Drink the cup He has assigned. Eat His bread. Rather than the temporary bread of earthly satisfaction, you are recipient of His promise:

"And Jesus said to them, 'I am the bread of life. He who comes to Me shall never hunger, and he who believes in Me shall never thirst.'" John 6:35

Your womb is now full of His harvest. You are becoming so fruitful that you are surrounded with lilies, not thorns.

"Blessed is the man whose strength is in You, whose heart is set on pilgrimage. As they pass through the Valley of Baca, they make it a spring; the rain also covers it with pools. They go from strength to strength; each one appears before God in Zion." Psalm 84:5-7

A heart set on pilgrimage, dancing between two camps, claims His strength. Learn as you pass through the valley of weeping, to make it a spring and to allow tears, brokenness, imperfections, and the gaps in life to pour out as life-giving water.

"Those who sow in tears shall reap in joy. He who continually goes forth weeping, bearing seed for sowing, shall doubtless come again with rejoicing, bringing his sheaves with him." Psalm 126:5-6

As Your blood flows in my veins, so Your body's brokenness is my bread of life. I was crucified with you, and I no longer live, but You live in me. And as I continually surrender my life, my ambitions, the chains that would bind me to death, I exchange them for Your eternal, passionate colorful Life.

As the bread of Your body was first blessed, then broken, then given out, so hold me, bless me, break me, and make me Your taste of the covenant — Your life in me.

"And as they were eating, Jesus took bread, blessed and broke it, and gave it to the disciples and said, 'Take, eat; this is My body.' Then He took the cup, and gave thanks, and gave it to them, saying, 'Drink from it, all of you. For this is My blood of the new covenant, which is shed for many for the remission of sins. But I say to you, I will not drink of this fruit of the vine from now on until that day when I drink it new with you in My Father's kingdom.'" Matthew 26:26-29

Remember Me. I will remember You.

SEARCH ME, O GOD, AND KNOW MY HEART.

* *"For as the heavens are high above the earth, so great is His mercy toward those who fear Him; as far as the east is from the west, so far has He removed our transgressions from us." Psalm 103:11-12*

- *Thank you for Your inexhaustible mercies. Show me anything I must confess and allow You to remove.*

- *"But if we walk in the light as He is in the light, we have fellowship with one another, and the blood of Jesus Christ His Son cleanses us from all sin. If we say that we have no sin, we deceive ourselves, and the truth is not in us. If we confess our sins, He is faithful and just to forgive us our sins and to cleanse us from all unrighteousness." I John 1:7-9*

- *O Lamb of God, thank You for Your cleansing blood. As You cleanse me from all sin, show me if I in any way allow or invite unrighteousness into my life.*

- *"For if you forgive men their trespasses, your heavenly Father will also forgive you. But if you do not forgive men their trespasses, neither will your Father forgive your trespasses." Matthew 6:14-15*

- As I receive afresh Your forgiveness, is there anyone I have yet to forgive?

- "Therefore if you bring your gift to the altar, and there remember that your brother has something against you, leave your gift there before the altar, and go your way. First be reconciled to your brother, and then come and offer your gift." Matthew 5:23-24

- Is there anyone from whom I should ask forgiveness, anyone hurt by me?

- "Then Jesus said to them, 'Most assuredly, I say to you, Moses did not give you the bread from heaven, but My Father gives you the true bread from heaven. For the bread of God is He who comes down from heaven and gives life to the world.' Then they said to Him, 'Lord, give us this bread always.'" John 6:32-34

- *Is there any bread in my mouth that does not belong? Am I eating bread that does not bring life?*

- *"But Jesus answered and said, 'You do not know what you ask. Are you able to drink the cup that I am about to drink, and be baptized with the baptism that I am baptized with?'" Matthew 20:22*

- *Describe to me the cup You are asking me to drink.*

- *As Your body was broken to bring life, so I allow You to break me that Your life would make me a life-giving blessing to others. Lift my eyes from any hurt or sacrifice of mine and fix them on Your eyes as You look at me and say, "This is My beloved daughter, in whom I am well pleased."*

Come, Fill the Gap

DAY 25

His Reservoir

Ah! How often, Christians, hath God kissed you at the beginning of prayer, and spoken peace to you in the midst of prayer, and filled you with joy and assurance upon the close of prayer! - Thomas Brooks[105]

SONG OF SONGS 7:3-13

"Your two breasts are like two fawns, twins of a gazelle. Your neck is like an ivory tower, your eyes like the pools in Heshbon by the gate of Bath Rabbim. Your nose is like the tower of Lebanon which looks toward Damascus. Your head crowns you like Mount Carmel, and the hair of your head is like purple; a king is held captive by your tresses. How fair and how pleasant you are, O love, with your delights!

This stature of yours is like a palm tree, and your breasts like its clusters. I said, 'I will go up to the palm tree, I will take hold of its branches.' Let now your breasts be like clusters of the vine, the fragrance of your breath like apples, and the roof of your mouth like the best wine. The wine goes down smoothly for my beloved, moving gently the lips of sleepers.

I am my Beloved's, and His desire is toward me. Come, my Beloved, let us go forth to the field; let us lodge in the villages. Let us get up early to the vineyards; let us see if the vine has budded, whether the grape blossoms are open, and the pomegranates are in bloom. There I will give you my love. The mandrakes give off a fragrance, and at our gates are pleasant fruits, all manner, new and old, which I have laid up for you, my Beloved."

Literary Treasures, as in Day 20, will be peppered throughout today's devotion, so we savor their riches bite by bite and let our soul sing with each flavor.

"Your two breasts are like two fawns, twins of a gazelle." Song of Solomon 7:3

Breasts are a sign of maturity and nourishment, as with a nursing mother. At this point, she has matured so much that her breasts can feed others His milk, He, who is repeatedly described as a gazelle. (2:9, 2:17, and 8:14) He used the exact same description in chapter 4, verse 5, as He often speaks truth, even before it is visible. Outside of time, He knew before you were conceived who you would become. "Before I formed you in the womb I knew you; before you were born I sanctified you; I ordained you." (Jeremiah 1:5) What did you enjoy when you were five years old? When did you feel most alive at eight? He magnificently wove together the unique textures of talent, joy, and purpose in you, and as you mature into His likeness, they increasingly exhibit His flavor.

"Your neck is like an ivory tower, your eyes like the pools in Heshbon by the gate of Bath Rabbim. Your nose is like the tower of Lebanon which looks toward Damascus." Song of Solomon 7:4

Your neck is like an ivory tower (Song of Solomon 7:4) whereas in chapter 4, verse 4, it was *like the tower of David, built for an armory*. Some suggest it alludes to the tower built by Solomon, mentioned in I Kings 7:2. Whereas beloved David was a man of war, his son Solomon was one of peace. Many of David's battles he did not choose; they were assigned by the Lord as necessities for establishing the kingdom. Similarly, many of your battles in life were required to establish His Kingdom in you. And though Earth will be a battleground until He establishes His physical reign, some strivings do cease with maturity. Think of something you struggled with early on which is much less of an issue now. And He shows us how:

The *pool* literally means *a reservoir, a resting place*.[106] Heshbon was the residence of the Amorite king Shihon (Numbers 21:25), and "Bath-rabbim" *daughter of a multitude* or *a crowded thoroughfare*.[107] In other words, among enemies and in the midst of crowds, you have found a resting place, a reservoir from which to draw peace.

After communion, savoring the unsearchable wonders His blessed, broken body and poured out wine purchased, there is peace. The clamor of the world subsides; the cravings of our own nature are still those of a baby, filled with mother's milk. Our eyes, since salvation, have been *doves* eyes. His purity and faithfulness were ours from our first breath in His kingdom. While innocent faith is endearing, there is a deeper peace we cannot manufacture. It is the peace of having been blessed, broken, and given out for Him. Having faced insurmountable inadequacies, having heard His call and been reluctant, having been washed by His forgiveness, and having been embraced again after failures, our souls know an experiential knowledge that indeed He covers every gap. Our eyes become a reservoir, a resting place **where fears are stilled and strivings cease**.

During my last conversation with my Brita, I had to ask her forgiveness. She herself had been a reservoir of Him as long as I had known her. Not only her eyes, but her voice has always been to me like fresh splashes from the pools of Heshbon. And in her slow death from cancer, this peace has been a **gift to me. I didn't even need to ask Him; He just handed it to me like a security blanket.** And when she described being ravished by something worse than the worst stomach virus, which repeatedly kept her violently vomiting for days on end, she would say, **It's just my body. My soul is snuggled into Jesus' arms.**

But when the person she loves dearest in the world was also suddenly dying from cancer, an uncharacteristic anxiety took hold. Yes, her loved one was also in the safe arms of Jesus, but her grown children were not. How would they react, if in fact, she died from this? Would they turn on God in anger and disappointment? This was tearing at Brita more than the excruciating physical pain. And in my immaturity, I regurgitated every cliché I could think of to comfort her. But I could hear they didn't work. As I hung up, I knew I had blown it, but I wasn't sure how to correct it. She could barely talk at all. Should I use what little strength she had to soothe my own conscience?

I waited a few days, before leaving a message alluding to my clumsiness, but not directly apologizing. Time with her now was so precious; I didn't want to waste it in any way. But after a week, I couldn't bear it anymore; I called, and she had the strength to pick up. The more morphine she took over these cancer-ridden years, the more frank she became. Her diplomacy filter eroded, and I loved her more than ever, as her raw thoughts were shared with me.

Brita, I'm so sorry! I was overriding your signals to be still, to respect your grief without shouting my inexperienced wisdom at you, I pleaded. *I do remember that!* she replied. *And you're right; clichés like that aren't all that helpful when our hearts are cut open and bleeding. We need balm from another source. But of course I forgive you; I know your heart.* These were the sweet last words to me from my beloved, lifelong mentor.

We need balm from another source.

"But God has revealed them to us through His Spirit. For the Spirit searches all things, yes, and the deep things of God. For what man knows the things of a man except the spirit of the man which is in him? Even so no one knows the things of God except the Spirit of God. Now we have received, not the spirit of the world, but the Spirit who is from God, that we might know the things that have been freely given to us by God. These things we also speak, not in words which man's wisdom teaches but which the Holy Spirit teaches, comparing spiritual things with spiritual." I Corinthians 2:10-13

Lush, tropical trees dip their roots in the canal behind our church building, a joy to the eye, yet bearing no fruit. The water in the canal always has movement - perhaps from the bottles and cans and wrappers constantly thrown in. The churn of trash and mud and seawater produces a color which admits no name.

The pools of Heshbon are placid, still.

When we are still, the mud settles on the bottom, and the water clears up. Had I been still while listening to Brita's concerns, perhaps I could have drawn balm from His Living waters for her, instead of pouring out the muddy ones of my own rushed life.

Quiet my mind, Lord. Make me still before You.

As you read for yourself the colorful passion spoken over you, drink it into your most unreached places:

"Your head crowns you like Mount Carmel, and the hair of your head is like purple; a king is held captive by your tresses. How fair and how pleasant you are, O love, with your delights!" Song of Solomon 7:5-6

As the head of the church (Colossians 1:18), Jesus crowns us with royalty. (**purple**; see 1 Peter 2:9) Mount Carmel, literally meaning *God's vineyard, is a coastal mountain range in northern Israel stretching from the Mediterranean Sea towards the southeast. Archaeologists have discovered ancient wine and oil presses at various locations on Mt. Carmel.*[108]

Be sure to grasp what is communicated in these somewhat obscure treasures. When He is your head, His royalty is bestowed on you and you become His vineyard, rich in the new wine of His Spirit and anointing oil which breaks the yokes of this world (see Isaiah 10:27). When you live in His identity, your ivory neck erect, not in pride, but in freedom, it captivates Him. Take it in; this Living Word fertilizes a vineyard like nothing else. "These things I have spoken to you, that My joy may remain in you, and that your joy may be full." John 15:11

"This stature of yours is like a palm tree, and your breasts like its clusters. I said, 'I will go up to the palm tree, I will take hold of its branches. Let now your breasts be like clusters of the vine, the fragrance of your breath like apples, and the roof of your mouth like the best wine. The wine goes down smoothly for my beloved, moving gently the lips of sleepers.'" Song of Solomon 7:7-9

There is no way not to sense the sexuality implied. Just this once, I must quote Mae West: *Sex is an emotion in motion*[109] All creation expresses His emotion; He designed it as a visual testimony to His invisible reality. "The heavens declare the glory of God; and the firmament shows His handiwork. Day unto day utters speech, and night unto night reveals knowledge. There is no speech nor language where their voice is not heard. Their line has gone out through all the earth, and their words to the end of the world. In them He has set a tabernacle for the sun, which is like a bridegroom coming out of his chamber." Psalm 19:1-5

The Palm tree was a symbol of triumphant joy when, for a brief moment, Jerusalem acknowledged her true King. (John 12:13) It will be again when we finally worship Him freely before the throne. (Revelation 7:9) Referring to the New Jerusalem where we will be one bride, He says, "Rejoice with Jerusalem, and be glad with her, all you who love her; rejoice for joy with her, all you who mourn for her; that you may feed and be satisfied with the consolation of her bosom, that you may drink deeply and be delighted with the abundance of her glory." Isaiah 66:10-11

There will be the complete consolation for which the whole creation groans, but "let now your breasts be like clusters of the vine, the fragrance of your breath like apples, and the roof of your mouth like the best wine." (Song of Solomon 7:8b) For now, you, God's vineyard, be the breath of His Holy Spirit on this earth and let your words be like His sweetest wine, His life-giving kiss to the *sleepers*. Song of Solomon 7:9

"Death and life are in the power of the tongue, and those who love it will eat its fruit." Proverbs 18:21

"I am my Beloved's, and his desire is toward me. Come, my Beloved, let us go forth to the field; let us lodge in the villages." Song of Solomon 7:10 -11

Deeper and deeper in the dance of love, they are leaving Jerusalem to lodge in the villages. They are to lodge there, making themselves at home away from Home. We are pilgrims in the Valley of Weeping (Psalm 84:6), not Home yet, but not at home here, either. The paradox: in order to reach our lost ones or whomever He sends us out of Jerusalem to reach, we must leave the old life behind. It must be His way: to life, we must die, to reach people we must be willing to lose them. It requires courage. It commands faith. But what's the alternative?

"And everyone who has left houses or brothers or sisters or father or mother or wife or children or lands, for My name's sake, shall receive a hundredfold, and inherit eternal life." Matthew 19:29

To my **Jerusalem**, it was a big deal when I gave up flamenco. **El duende**, the spirit of gypsy flamenco was so entrenched in me that I think some wondered if there would be anything of me left without it. Would I just be an empty shell? Twenty years later, the artists I so full-bloodedly loved and love, still scratch their heads, convinced I made an unexplainable mistake. And I knew they would, and I had to do it anyway. I had to die to the relationships that mattered most to me, hoping and praying that some day, He might make me a chariot to that people. But I had to go forth to the fields where His love drew me without strings attached. He would fill the gap.

Fast forward twenty years, and the shell flamenco left behind is not empty. Inside the vacuum I gave my Lover now grows a lush, expansive, enclosed garden, because He gives beauty for ashes, because He longs more for my fruitfulness than I do, because He promised that trees with roots in His Water will bear healing fruit for the nations.

Between the first Garden of Eden and the New Earth, there is us. We are His garden Enclosed.

"He shall be like a tree planted by the rivers of water, that brings forth its fruit in its season, whose leaf also shall not wither; and whatever he does shall prosper." Psalm 1:3

"And he showed me a pure river of water of life, clear as crystal, proceeding from the throne of God and of the Lamb. In the middle of its street, and on either side of the river, was the tree of life, which bore twelve fruits, each tree yielding its fruit every month. The leaves of the tree were for the healing of the nations." Revelation 22:1-2

"Let us get up early to the vineyards; let us see if the vine has bud- ded, whether the grape blossoms are open, and the pomegranates are in bloom. There I will give you my love. The mandrakes give off a fragrance, and at our gates are pleasant fruits, all manner, new and old, which I have laid up for you, my Beloved." Song of Solomon 7:12-13

Known as an aphrodisiac, **mandrakes** were **supposed to exhilarate the spirits and excite love**.[110] In Scripture, it is only mentioned here and in Genesis 30:14-16, when Rachel was desperate for children, for a fruitful womb. Without minimizing the agony of barrenness, we know with full assurance that He desires and enables us to be fruitful.

"You did not choose Me, but I chose you and appointed you that you should go and bear fruit, and that your fruit should remain, that whatever you ask the Father in My name He may give you." John 15:16

Every time you attend someone in His Spirit, you lay up fruit for your Beloved. "And the King will answer and say to them, 'Assuredly,

I say to you, inasmuch as you did it to one of the least of these My brethren, you did it to Me.'" Matthew 25:40

SEARCH ME, O GOD, AND KNOW MY HEART.

* *"Be still, and know that I am God." (Palm 46:10) Show me the noises of my life and the activities that overpower Your still, small voice. Show me how to dim their influence to magnify Yours.*

* *"But we all, with unveiled face, beholding as in a mirror the glory of the Lord, are being transformed into the same image from glory to glory, just as by the Spirit of the Lord." 2 Corinthians 3:18*

* *What are You transforming me into? How and when do I best reflect Your glory?*

* *"Thus says the LORD: 'Heaven is My throne, And earth is My footstool. Where is the house that you will build Me? And where is the place of My rest?*

*For all those things My hand has made, and all those
things exist,' Says the LORD. 'But on this one will
I look: on him who is poor and of a contrite spirit,
and who trembles at My word.'" Isaiah 66:1-2*

- *Come, Lord, make Your home with me and
  draw me deeper into Your Word that I may
  enlarge Your resting place in me.*

- *Is there anything in my life that remains
  alive, but should be dead?*

- *This is My commandment, that you love one another as
  I have loved you. (John 15:12) Show me whom and how.*

- *I will follow you anywhere. I will tend to
  Your vineyard with You. Anywhere You
  lead, there I will give You my love.*

DAY 26
The Beautiful Yearning

The yearning for You is beyond a cry
Remembrances from my origin
Fragrances, sounds, from before we died
Calling from deepest within

Deliver in me the colors so bright
The beauty we all seem to miss
Transform me to be this breath-taking sight
Of the Bride You ache to kiss

Teach me to love You without any cover
Without any duty or fear
Teach me to receive You, Heavenly Lover
To just realize: You are here!

SONG OF SOLOMON 8:1-3

"Oh, that you were like my brother, who nursed at my mother's breasts! If I should find you outside, I would kiss you; I would not be despised. I would lead you and bring you into the house of my mother, she who used

to instruct me. I would cause you to drink of spiced wine, of the juice of my pomegranate. His left hand is under my head, and his right hand embraces me."

LITERARY TREASURES

Do not be alarmed at the shift from lover to brother. John Gill sheds light on it: *"Christ is the Church's brother by virtue of his incarnation, or the assumption of her nature; they are nearly allied in the bonds of consanguinity; he is of the same flesh and blood with her; and she is flesh of his flesh, and bone of his bone; there is a very great nearness, affinity and likeness between them, for 'in all things it behooved him to be made like unto his brethren' and it is upon this score that he becomes a brother to them."*[111]

No, this is not an incestuous wish! There is not the slightest shadow of darkness in Him! (See James 1:17) The gift of this Song is as good and perfect as every gift from the Father of lights. The progression of our journey from the first "Let Him kiss me with the kisses of His mouth" (Song of Solomon 1:2) has been one of maturing-in-love-ness. As a seasoned married couple embodies brother-sister, husband-wife, father-mother roles, even more so does our relationship with the multifaceted Creator. As a diamond reflects the colors of the rainbow, so does His covenant with us reflect limitless nuances of His brilliant radiance.

"Into the house of my mother, she who used to instruct me" (Song of Solomon 8:2) seems so clearly to refer to the church, the house and the fellowship in which we receive instruction. Thus the **spiced wine** appears to be communion, that sacred, mysterious oneness He ordained as a ritual to remember Him - to become one with His sacrifice.

The embrace in verse 3 is a verbatim repetition of the first full embrace in chapter 2, verse 6. He pleasures in these repetitions as they are really reassurances. The patriarchs used both hands for blessing (see Genesis 38:14), though the blessings differed. The priests in Leviticus 14 used their left hand to hold the oil used symbolically to cleanse and atone for sin. Both His hands are engaged in blessing and cleansing you. His embrace is complete, and "no one is able to snatch them out of My Father's hand." John 10:29

COME, FILL THE GAP

Oh, if only I could indeed touch You! If only You were physical as I!

You awake in me a life that cannot fully live here. You spark desires in my deepest core that yearn to burn brighter than they fully can now. I taste the life-giving drops of Your waters, Your "spiced wine" (Song of Solomon 8:2) and even as they satisfy, they leave me thirsty for more, more, more – the longing to fulfill my design!

Anyone who has tasted a genuine kiss of the one who makes their heart beat harder or stop beating at all, knows the escalating pull towards making love. It is a natural pull; it reflects the gravitational draw of our Lover towards us. Soon it will wrench us right out of here; meanwhile, it throbs in our chests as a beautiful ache.

Consider that the highest ecstasy of physical union is designed as a foretaste of a much higher joy in His arms as His bride. Our reference point is so polluted that we barely imagine the absolute freedom of Adam and Eve when they were naked and unashamed before the Fall. Experience since then has become increasingly distorted, dwarfed, deformed. Take Him at His Word. He is our Groom and we are the Bride.

"Then they said to her, 'Woman, why are you weeping?' She said to them, 'Because they have taken away my Lord, and I do not know where they have laid Him.' Now when she had said this, she turned around and saw Jesus standing there, and did not know that it was Jesus. Jesus said to her, 'Woman, why are you weeping? Whom are you seeking?' She, supposing Him to be the gardener, said to Him, 'Sir, if You have carried Him away, tell me where You have laid Him, and I will take Him away.' Jesus said to her, 'Mary!' She turned and said to Him, 'Rabboni!' (which is to say, Teacher). Jesus said to her, 'Do not cling to Me, for I have not yet ascended to My Father; but go to My brethren and say to them, 'I am ascending to My Father and your Father, and to My God and your God.'" John 20:13-17

How it must have pained Him to place that boundary between them. But for now, boundaries are necessary, as we are not free from shadow as is our Lover of light. We live in this gap between where we hear His familiar Voice caressing our name, but are unable to caress His face. It hurts. It's as though we have receptors designed to be fused to His, and He is grazing them, but not lips to lips connecting. Let the gap draw you towards Him, not away in disappointment, not to available substitutes! Hunger is better unmet than met by poison! It is better to weep like Mary, unaware that He is listening, thinking Him absent when He is not, than to laugh the brazen laugh of a seared conscience in the arms of an illegitimate lover. "Better is one day in His house than a thousand elsewhere." Psalm 84:10

SEARCH ME, O GOD, AND KNOW MY HEART

- *"One thing I have desired of the LORD, that will I seek: That I may dwell in the house of the LORD all the days of my life, to behold the beauty of the LORD, and to inquire in His temple." Psalm 27:4*

- *Oh, Lord, again and again I ask, let me see Your beauty. Show me any attraction or affection that illegitimately seduces me.*

- *"O God, You are my God; Early will I seek You; My soul thirsts for You; My flesh longs for You In a dry and thirsty land where there is no water." Psalm 63:1*

- *What am I prone to doing when my thirst goes unmet?*

- *"Blessed are you who hunger now, for you shall be filled. Blessed are you who weep now, for you shall laugh." Luke 6:21*

- *When I am weeping, do I turn towards You or away?*

- *What do I truly hunger for?*

- *Oh You, "Who led them by the right hand of Moses, with His glorious arm, dividing the water before them to make for Himself an everlasting name," (Isaiah 63:12) divide the waters before me as I move towards Your Promised Land. Use me to magnify Your everlasting Name!*

- *"Let him kiss me with the kisses of his mouth - for your love is better than wine." Song of Solomon 1:2*

- *When I long for Your kisses and I don't realize how near You are, say my name in a way I know it's You. My hunger and thirst lies open before You. Unless a gift is from You, I don't want! Come, fill the gap.*

- *Spend time today exploring your longings and then giving them to Him. 'To sanctify' means to set apart for Him; sanctify whatever pours out from your depths, as you write now. Don't censor what comes; instead hand it to Him.*

- *Lord, all my desire is before You; and my sighing is not hidden from You. Psalms 38:9*

- *"The sacrifices of God are a broken spirit, A broken and a contrite heart - These, O God, You will not despise." Psalms 51:17*

Come, Fill the Gap

DAY 27
Who is this?

W estley: *Hear this now: I will always come for you.*
Buttercup: **But how can you be sure?**
Westley: *This is true love - you think this happens every day?*[112]

SONG OF SOLOMON 8:5

"Who is this coming up from the wilderness, leaning upon her beloved? I awakened you under the
apple tree. There your mother brought you forth;
there she who bore you brought you forth."

LITERARY TREASURES

Here appears another poetic repetition with a twist. In chapter 3, verse 6 she asked, "Who is this coming out of the wilderness"; in response He asked, "Who is she who looks forth as the morning?" (Song of Solomon 6:10) Now a relative exclaims, "Who is this coming up from the wilderness, leaning upon her beloved?"

The **wilderness** might imply a pasture for grazing or a desert. The same Hebrew word[113] is used for the place Hagar fled from Sarai's wrath and was later sent by Abram. (Genesis 21:14) It is not the word used for Jesus' 40 days of temptation in Matthew 4, which implies **lonesome, desolate**.[114] We will never experience the loneliness He had to endure. Neither Hagar nor the Shulamite escaped the comfort of Emanuel, God with us.

Strangely, the Hebrew word[115] for **leaning** upon Him is only used this one place in the entire Old Testament. It simply means **reclining** and bears association to the beloved disciple John confidently leaning into Jesus' bosom, unafraid to ask the difficult question. John 13:23-25

Awakened[116] denotes the ideas of **opening the eyes** as well as **stirring up**. It is the word used in Deuteronomy 32:11: "As an eagle stirs up its nest, hovers over its young, spreading out its wings, taking them up, carrying them on its wings." Oh, the consistency of God's Word! She is leaning on her beloved; she is carried on His wings.

About the **apple tree**, the commentary writes, *Found ruined under the forbidden tree (Genesis 3: 22-24); restored under the shadow of Jesus Christ crucified, 'the green tree' (Luke 23:31), fruit-bearing by the cross (Isaiah 53:11; John 12:24). 'Born again by the Holy Ghost' 'there' (Ezekiel 16:3-6). In this verse, her dependence, in the similar verse, Song of Solomon 3:6, His omnipotence to support her, are brought out. Deuteronomy 33:26"*[117]

COME, FILL THE GAP

Who is this, trusting her beloved so completely? It is someone who has learned to sink her whole weight into Him, not holding anything back. It is someone who from experience knows Who He is. In this, as in all relationships, there is no substitute for time's proclamation of trustworthiness.

The fresh sweetness of young love is precious, but untested. Though soaring in unparalleled rush, invincible and arrogant, young lovers barely know each other or themselves. In the sunshine season, they have no idea of the strength of the flesh, the intelligence of the adversary, or the dark shadows of curse under which all creation writhes. Nor should they; it is not their season.

Mature love on the other hand, has weathered those very situations. Stripped to the core, forced to answer hard questions, illusion and misimpression are exposed. Instead, the truth glimmers as a polished diamond: that He is faithful when we are not,[118] that love covers a multitude of wrongs,[119] and that His mercy is new every morning.[120] As with the apostle Paul, it is the fiery trials which bring us gravitas. As with Nathaniel who surrendered to Jesus' kingship and believed in a small thing[121], and was thus promised he would see greater things, trust crystallizes in experience.

"The LORD did not set His love on you nor choose you because you were more in number than any other people, for you were the least of all peoples; but because the LORD loves you, and because He would keep the oath which He swore to your fathers, the LORD has brought you out with a mighty hand, and redeemed you from the house of bondage, from the hand of Pharaoh king of Egypt. Therefore know that the LORD your God, He is God, the faithful God who keeps covenant and mercy for a thousand generations with those who love Him and keep His commandments." Deuteronomy 7:7-9

If, when we fear the overwhelming storms of life, when we bear the pain we thought would rend us in pieces, we turn towards him and not away, we will find that those mighty hands do protect and free our soul from bondage. When we learn to weep into him, to bury our breaking hearts in His chest, we allow Him to bear the full weight of our existence.

We are no longer two separate identities. As in the original design, before the fall when there was no hiding, we become One. Our Creator's heavenly ways are so mind-bogglingly different from ours! Just as we must lose our lives to live, just as it is more blessed to give than receive, so we gain our true identity when we lose ourselves in Him. Those around us recognize it. We become whom He had in mind when we were skillfully wrought in secret.

"Your eyes saw my substance, being yet unformed. And in Your book they all were written, the days fashioned for me, when as yet there were none of them." Psalm 139:16

Solomon wrote, "Thorns and snares are in the way of the perverse; he who guards his soul will be far from them. Train up a child in the way he should go, and when he is old he will not depart from it." (Proverbs 22:5-6) We must reject any fear that when our Father trains us (however He might choose) it is to keep us from the thorns and secret snares strewn like landmines in the way of the perverse. The word for perverse means *corrupted*[122] and He explains it thus: *They have corrupted themselves; they are not His children, because of their blemish: A perverse and crooked generation.*[123] It is back to the teeth of faith (Song of Solomon 4:2). It is always back to believing that He is good, no matter what.

"No temptation has overtaken you except such as is common to man; but God is faithful, who will not allow you to be tempted beyond what you are able, but with the temptation will also make the way of escape, that you may be able to bear it." (I Corinthians 10:13) The way of escape leads out of the wilderness.

As we lean upon our Beloved, while coming out of the wilderness, we walk into the pages of the days fashioned for us. My parents put it like this: **When you were a little girl, we perceived who you were. But somewhere in childhood, you lost your way, and we didn't recognize you. You became like the people you admired, but you lost yourself. Now we know you again**." Granted, my relieved mother wasn't initially quite sure if it was Robert or Jesus who found me - but as her years brought my man from a pedestal to a more realistic place by my side, my mother drew closer to the Redeemer of both her daughters.

"Who is like You, O LORD, among the gods? Who is like You, glorious in holiness, fearful in praises, doing wonders?" Exodus 15:11

Leaning on these mighty hands, these eagles' wings, breathing in the life of Him who is "merciful and gracious, longsuffering, and abounding in goodness and truth, keeping mercy for thousands, forgiving iniquity and transgression and sin,"[24] it is foolish and naïve to attempt to steer Him our own way. The more we are aware of the shielding protection and thrilling adventure, the more we welcome His exclusivity. "So the LORD alone led him, and there was no foreign god with him." Deuteronomy 32:12

SEARCH ME, O GOD, AND KNOW MY HEART.

* *"Before I formed you in the womb I knew you; before you were born I sanctified you." Jeremiah 1:5a*

- Describe yourself when you were a young child.

- What caused you to lose your way?

- "Where can I go from Your Spirit? Or where can I flee from Your presence? If I ascend into heaven, You are there; if I make my bed in hell, behold, You are there. If I take the wings of the morning, and dwell in the uttermost parts of the sea, even there Your hand shall lead me, and Your right hand shall hold me." Psalm 139:7-10

- Am I holding on to escape routes? Show me situations where I flee Your Spirit.

- "You in Your mercy have led forth the people whom You have redeemed; You have guided them in Your strength to Your holy habitation." (Exodus 15:13) As I am coming out of the wilderness, leaning on You, talk to me about the pages in my book I have yet to step into.

- *"O LORD, You have searched me and known me. You know my sitting down and my rising up; You understand my thought afar off. You comprehend my path and my lying down, and are acquainted with all my ways. For there is not a word on my tongue, but behold, O LORD, You know it altogether. You have hedged me behind and before, and laid Your hand upon me. Such knowledge is too wonderful for me; it is high, I cannot attain it." Psalm 139:1-6*

Come, Fill the Gap

DAY 28
Sealed, Engraved, Established

He felt now that he was not simply close to her, but that he did not know where he ended and she began. - Leo Tolstoy

SONG OF SOLOMON 8:6-7

"Set me as a seal upon your heart, as a seal upon your arm; for love is as strong as death, jealousy as cruel as the grave; its flames are flames of fire, a most vehement flame. Many waters cannot quench love, nor can the floods drown it. If a man would give for love all the wealth of his house, it would be utterly despised."

LITERARY TREASURES

Seal is a *signature ring, a signet.*[125] It is the word used for the high priest's golden engravings, carrying the names of the children of Israel.[126] Even so, our High priest carries our names upon His heart, upon His arm, and even in the palm of His hands. *See, I have inscribed you on the palms of My hands; your walls are continually before Me.*[127] As in Song of Solomon 8:5, she was *leaning* on Him, that is, her arm on His arm, her head on His bosom; so she prays now that before they part, her impression may be engraven both on His heart and His arm, answering to His love and His power.[128]

The word for *strong* implies *vehement, harsh*[129] just like death. Costly love may be foreign to our culture, but it is the very heart of the Gospel (see John 10:15 & 15:13). The King James Version translates the jealousy simile *the coals thereof are coals of fire. Many waters* and *floods* are the obvious contrast to these flames.

COME, FILL THE GAP

Each divine Word waits, heavy-laden with meaning, but for a moment, just take in the fiery intensity of the sound...

We are sealed by the Holy Spirit, engaged, guaranteed our King is coming soon on a white horse to collect us and spirit us away to happily ever after. "Now He who establishes us with you in Christ and has anointed us is God, who also has sealed us and given us the Spirit in our hearts as a guarantee." (2 Corinthians 1:21-22) Do not allow the wait to douse and drown out your desire. Instead, let his Word so inflame the longing that it blazes brighter and brighter in this night.

"In Him you also trusted, after you heard the word of truth, the gospel of your salvation; in whom also, having believed, you were sealed with the Holy Spirit of promise, who is the guarantee of our inheritance until the redemption of the purchased possession, to the praise of His glory." Ephesians 1:13-14

My mother's name is engraved inside the gold wedding band on my father's finger - not on the outside for show, but on the inside where it touches his skin. It is a private seal. Her name was Eva. She is buried in a pristine garden in the heart of the old village where he lives. It is an elevated garden, the center of attention. There she lies with his name against her finger. A kiss on her cold forehead was the last time he touched her. **Love is as strong as death.**

Why is jealousy as cruel as the grave? In this Alice-In-Wonderland, upside-down nightmare, we have made jealousy a villain. And here God's word characterizes it as **cruel as the grave**. Oprah famously exclaimed that it was when she heard that our God is a jealous God she wrote Him off. What associations does the word **jealous** bring to you? Does it evoke some clingy, possessive, controlling, person plunging tooth and claw into a victimized lover?

My old camp views it this way, and so did I. But where the Spirit of the Lord is there is freedom (2 Corinthians 3:17). His jealousy must be something else entirely. Everything about Him is bountifully opposite the bloodless, colorless, blue-lipped kiss we call love. His jealousy is the kind that lays down His life to rescue His beloved. It sends men to war to protect women, children, truth, and beauty. It stops intruders.

Jealousy is cruel to Him! He is jealous FOR us, ON our behalf, lest someone kill, steal, or destroy the abundant life He died to provide. As we await the thunderous hooves of His alabaster steed, our days might be glorious, and as we turn our faces towards Him, the more we'll be like Him. Never allow lesser versions or political correctness to steal the heroism of real, unapologetic jealousy. Behold and beseech its fiery glory.

"But we all, with unveiled face, beholding as in a mirror the glory of the Lord, are being transformed into the same image from glory to glory, just as by the Spirit of the Lord." 2 Corinthians 3:18

"They shall see His face, and His name shall be on their foreheads. There shall be no night there: they need no lamp nor light nor sun, for the Lord God gives them light." Revelation 22:4-5

"Many waters cannot quench love, nor can the floods drown it. If a man would give for love all the wealth of his house, it would be utterly despised." Song of Solomon 8:7

Love and jealousy are vehement flames, and many waters, no matter the substance, cannot quench the inferno.

When governments attempt to crucify Christianity, it rises from the grave! Meeting in secret, at night, at terrible risk, the Chinese house church movement is unparalleled in its growth and tenacity. I wonder which flames burn brighter. Persecution in Jerusalem's first church was God's hand scattering the seeds to the whole world. **Don't pray for our persecution to end**, our Chinese brothers are famous for saying, **pray that yours will bear fruit when it comes**.

Perhaps we shrink back in fear at such audacity. Why would anyone wish persecution on anyone else? The faces of these martyrs shine with a freedom we hardly appreciate. The fires of trial and terror have burned away the dross from their countenance. They know that their own strength is nothing. And in God's life-giving jealousy, he lifts them out of flesh and blood limitations into the life He intends for us all — the exchanged life — His for ours. It is not about who we are; it is all about Who He is. It is His life pulsing though our veins; it is His strength steadying our steps.

And therefore, our many weaknesses have not quenched His love. Nothing will; nothing can.

"Who shall bring a charge against God's elect? It is God who justifies. Who is he who condemns? It is Christ who died, and furthermore is also risen, who is even at the right hand of God, who also makes intercession for us. Who shall separate us from the love of Christ? Shall tribulation, or distress, or persecution, or famine, or nakedness, or peril, or sword? As it is written: 'FOR YOUR SAKE WE ARE KILLED ALL DAY LONG; WE ARE ACCOUNTED AS SHEEP FOR THE SLAUGHTER.' Yet in all these things we are more than conquerors through Him who loved us. For I am persuaded that neither death nor life, nor angels nor principalities nor powers, nor things present nor things to come, nor height nor depth, nor any other created thing, shall be able to separate us from the love of God which is in Christ Jesus our Lord." Romans 8:33-39

Take prisoner these Words; they will be life when trials and temptations contend to quench your love. The adversary, sly, intelligent, and observant of your defenses will enshroud himself in religious clothing and offer the world without the Cross. Watch out for small compromises that conveniently suggest an apparent alternative to the path God has placed before you. **Does it really matter that much?** You rationalize. It is almost obedience. **You don't have to be extreme. Did God really say...?** Genesis 3:1

In my dancing days, a position as a chorographer was offered me which, in the spirit of full disclosure, was above my pay grade. But risk taker to a fault, that was in itself a magnetic pull, not to mention the actors I would be working with. Yes, I knew that the play was saturated in sexuality, but it was also exceptionally poetic. I was seduced by the beautiful, rather than drawn to the true and the good. Dreadfully devoid of wisdom, I accepted on the spot.

At first, the inner voice of objection was vague enough that I could celebrate with honest excitement. But though a very green little sprout in the Vine of Jesus, I was grafted in. The pulse of His heart beat louder and louder, until I was miserable enough to stare my mistake in the face. And with the conviction that I had stepped outside His will came just enough strength to act on it. I knew when I reversed my decision that the director would not understand and would be offended at the implication that I now was **too holy** for her play. I had to do it anyway. And then His peace flooded over me, sweeter than any applause of men.

Satan offered the world to Jesus - "All this can be Yours if You will bow down and worship me" (Matthew 4:9) - with strings attached. But after He resisted, angels came and ministered to Him. As they did to me. As they will for you. As long as we are under the shadow of darkness, confirmation and commendation without the Cross will be offered to us. But our High Priest jealously intercedes for us that so we will not sell our soul. May we be like Moses, who didn't want the Promised Land without the Presence that makes it Paradise.

SEARCH ME, O GOD, AND KNOW MY HEART.

- *Set me as a seal upon Your heart,*
  as a seal upon you arm.

- *By Your establishing grace, I renew my vow to take*
  You as my constant friend, my faithful partner, and
  my love from this day forward. In the presence of Your
  Word and Your Spirit, I offer You my solemn vow to
  be Your faithful partner in sickness and in health, in
  good times and in bad, in joy as well as in sorrow. I
  promise to love and obey, to honor and respect You,
  to follow wherever You may lead, as Your Spirit gives
  me Grace - until You return or bring me Home.

DAY 29
Walls and Doors

*Never look down on a sister except
to pick her up. - Unknown*

Realizing how His love is everything, how she would now give everything for this love, her concern turns to her little sister who is less committed.

SONG OF SOLOMON 8:8-10

"We have a little sister, and she has no breasts. What shall we do for our sister in the day when she is spoken for? If she is a wall, we will build upon her a battlement of silver; and if she is a door, we will enclose her with boards of cedar. I am a wall, and my breasts like towers; then I became in his eyes as one who found peace."

LITERARY TREASURES

The Hebrew word for **wall** carries the tones of **to join; a wall of protection**.[130] It is **mind-blasting**, as I once heard a comedian say, how every one of His Living words indeed is pregnant with life. This wall is protective when she is joined with Him. All that loaded into one word!

The **battlement** also means **palace**[131] and is thus translated in the King James Version. It is a fortified, dignified habitation more than a place of war. Unlike human works unable to endure the fire of testing, silver will endure. "For no other foundation can anyone lay than that which is laid, which is Jesus Christ. Now if anyone builds on this foundation with gold, silver, precious stones, wood, hay, straw, each one's work will become clear; for the Day will declare it, because it will be revealed by fire; and the fire will test each one's work, of what sort it is." 1 Corinthians 3:11-13

Actually the Hebrew word translated **door** literally means **something swinging; that is the valve of a door**.[132] In other words, it is the movement of opening and closing that is the emphasis.

Notice the change of person in verse 10. In reflecting on the condition of this little sister, the Shulamite, herself more mature now, recognizes that joined to him in this protective wall, she has found peace. The Shulamite now embodies her name Shalom.

COME, FILL THE GAP

We have a little sister, and she is immature. What shall we do for her when she is spoken for, when suitors appeal for her affection?

Who are the little sisters in your life? Who are the sisters that don't yet bear His fruit and you sense that tempters are crouching at her door? She may not have the wisdom or strength to discern their intentions, but you sense that she is in danger. Maybe she is dating an unbeliever. Maybe she is giving herself away to him because, **He's** *going to marry me anyway* or *it's just not realistic to wait*. Maybe she just seems bored with life in the garden and is again pursuing the glitter of Egypt. And you're watching Egypt reclaim the decorated slave girl she used to be.

We never know what lies behind behavior. The older brother to the prodigal son, up until the celebration, behaved exemplary, but his heart was icy self-righteousness. His younger wayward brother, smelly and desperate, let his brokenness lead him to humility.

"For thus says the High and Lofty One Who inhabits eternity, whose name is Holy: 'I dwell in the high and holy place, with him who has a contrite and humble spirit, to revive the spirit of the humble, and to revive the heart of the contrite ones.'" Isaiah 57:15

The danger for older sisters is to become Pharisee watching the wretched tax collector from an illusion of superiority, of **thank you, God, that I'm better than he**.[133] Oh, watch out for that foxy attitude; it will ruin your vine! Of the two, the tax collector went home justified. Instead, remember how life looked through the eyes of your younger self. Do you remember the nausea of confusion? Do you recall being torn by expectations outside and bewildering emotions inside? *A sister can be seen as someone who is both ourselves and very much not ourselves - a special kind of double*. - Toni Morrison.

So what do we do with our little sister? First we find out if she is a wall or a door.

If she is a wall, if she still listens to her watchmen and respects His boundaries, she may be acting out of ignorance. Some childhoods, though possibly not redeemed by Jesus, still have His principles in place. Paul observed that some Gentiles obey the Law because it's written on their hearts. What is right and wrong in their world view is mostly in alignment with His. Others are far from it, and the most elementary principles of propriety are absent. These are just cultures; they do not define the quality of our hearts. If she is a wall and has the foundation of wanting to please Jesus, we build battlements of silver upon her.

"And if she is a door, we will enclose her with boards of cedar." Song of Solomon 8:9

 The word door refers to a swing door, as in a store, making her a public park, rather than an enclosed garden.

I have ever wanted to barricade some of my little sisters with solid cedar! When they come to me with the torn rags of their relationships or arrayed in the garments of Babylon, I hunger to shelter them in His safety, enfold and envelop them in soft blankets, and rock them like little babies.

And with my daughter, I do! With her, I am directly responsible and have the authority to enclose her, to discharge dangerous privileges, to protect her from herself.

But the God of free will does not allow me that authority with anyone else. So how can we enclose them with boards of cedar - that fragrant, strong, incorruptible wood? By prayer! We surround them with the effective, fervent prayers that rise before His throne day and night. And we are persistent with love.

Jesus and Satan see the same facts about us. Satan accuses. Jesus intercedes.

"For I am jealous for you with godly jealousy. For I have betrothed you to one husband, that I may present you as a chaste virgin to Christ." 2 Corinthians 11:2

"I am a wall, and my breasts like towers; then I became in his eyes as one who found peace." Song of Solomon 8:10

The best gift Brita ever gave me was her personal peace. She lived inside her walls with her Beloved for so many decades; He was her only Husband, and she a radiant bride. Her breasts were like towers. She gave milk to so many like me, and we now in turn are feeding others. Her serenity inspired me to fight for my own. I saw that it was fruitful, not selfish. It quickly convicted me when compromise had begun to erode it, because what I heard in her voice, the trust and surrender, made my soul sing in the way no professional singer could. I yearn for that eternal song to rise from my deepest core, but more than that, I live to accompany its melody with the souls of my little sisters.

SEARCH ME, O GOD, AND KNOW MY HEART.

- *"And the King will answer and say to them, 'Assuredly, I say to you, inasmuch as you did it to one of the least of these My brethren, you did it to Me.'" Matthew 25:40*

- *May I be a big sister like that to the many little sisters who need You. Who are my little sisters?*

- *How would You like me to love them for You?*

- *How would You like me to pray for them?*

DAY 30 : WALLS AND DOORS

DAY 30

Embrace me, Eternity

*I have now concentrated all my prayers into one,
and that one prayer is this, that I may die to self,
and live wholly to Him. -* C.H. Spurgeon[134]

In the last chapter of the Gospel of John, Jesus showed His disciples how to catch fish His way, and they were not able to draw in the net because of the multitude of the fish. He cooked them breakfast (those same fish He had provided) and perhaps the glow of the fire reminded Peter of the fire where he had warmed hands as he was denying Jesus. For each denial, He asked Peter, **Do you love Me?**, and each redeeming YES from Peter was followed by an exhortation, a plead, a commission, **feed My lambs, tend My sheep, feed My sheep.**[135]

In the last chapter of the Song of Solomon, to His beloved Shulamite, Shalom, the prince of Peace, showed us how to entrust our longings to Him, and our hearts became so full that we at times almost couldn't bear it. He then set us as a seal upon His heart, on Himself, as an unbroken wedding ring of death-defying love, protected by His jealousy. And as we thought of our little sister's fickle wall, we were reminded that our own wasn't always so strong, but now we have become in His eyes as one who found peace. As we have been established and secured with the help of our big sisters, as we have followed the footsteps of the flock, as He always urged us, there is one final admonition.

SONG OF SOLOMON 8:11-14

"Solomon had a vineyard at Baal Hamon; He leased the vineyard to keepers; everyone was to bring for its fruit a thousand silver coins. My own vineyard is before me. You, O Solomon, may have a thousand, and those who tend its fruit two hundred. You who dwell in the gardens, the companions listen for your voice – Let me hear it! Make haste, my beloved, and be like a gazelle or a young stag on the mountains of spices."

LITERARY TREASURES

Twenty-one times in the Gospels, Jesus, in an effort to open our earth-blind eyes to His reality, compares the Kingdom of Heaven to a vineyard (often in the context of leasing it to keepers and then watching for their faithfulness). **Baal Hamon** signifies **possessor of a multitude**.[136] Commentaries are divided over whether it refers to **the chief god of Carthage…a deity of sky and vegetation, depicted as a bearded older man with curling ram's horns**[137] or God Himself, as described in Isaiah 5:7: "For the vineyard of the LORD of hosts is the house of Israel, and the men of Judah are His pleasant plant." Either way, it is Solomon's vineyard, the vineyard of Shalom, and it certainly is planted on a planet otherwise in the darkness of this age.

About the numbers *thousand* and *two hundred*, it is suggested, *she will not keep it for herself, though so freely given to her, but for His use and glory...Or the 'two hundred' may mean a double tithe (two-tenths of the whole paid back by Jesus Christ) as the reward of grace for our surrender of all (the thousand) to Him...; then she and 'those that keep' are the same [Adelaide Newton]. But Jesus Christ pays back not merely two tithes, but His all for our all.*"[138]

COME, FILL THE GAP

The final notes in this Song from His heart tug at ours in a very direct way. His last Words are about our first fruits. "For where your treasure is, there your heart will be also." (Matthew 6:21) Specifically, our giving. Do we trust Him with that? As we ask Him to fill gaps, do we allow him access to this part of life? Anchored in His secure love, the Shulamite does. If this one stings, ask him why...

There are three conversions necessary: the conversion of the heart, mind, and the purse. - Martin Luther[139]

God has given us two hands - one to receive with and the other to give with. We are not cisterns made for hoarding; we are channels made for giving. - Billy Graham[140]

"You who dwell in the gardens, the companions listen for your voice - Let me hear it! Make haste, my beloved, and be like a gazelle or a young stag on the mountains of spices." Song of Solomon 8:13-14

Here I must again borrow from Jamieson, Faucett, and Brown for this rich concluding verse: *As there are four gardens, so four mountains, which form not mere images, as Gilead, Carmel, etc., but part of the structure of the Song: (1) Bether, or division (2:17), God's justice dividing us from God. (2) Those 'of leopards' (4:8), sin, the world, and Satan. (3) That 'of myrrh and aloes' (4:6, 4:14), the sepulchre of Calvary.*

(4) Those 'of spices,' here answering to 'the hill of frankincense' (4:6), where His soul was for the three days of His death, and heaven, where He is a High Priest now, offering incense for us on the fragrant mountain of His own finished work (Hebrews 4:14, Hebrews 7:25, Revelation 8:3-4); thus He surmounts the other three mountains, God's justice, our sin, death. The mountain of spices is as much greater than our sins, as heaven is higher than earth."[14]

Learning Hebrew words and ancient poetry, soaking in His Word and stretching our soul song towards Heaven, we funnel through the one simple truth of the Cross. If you remember nothing else of this book, remember that his Cross is enough. For every concern under Heaven, for every flutter of the spirit, His cross is sufficient. Discard those affairs that attempt to replace the cross in your life and enter into the covenant prayer, **Come, fill the gap**.

"SEARCH ME, O GOD, AND KNOW MY HEART; TRY ME, AND KNOW MY ANXIETIES." PSALM 139:23

- *You, oh Savior may have all of my garden, - and those who tend its fruits, my church, the missionaries in my life, those in chains for Your Kingdom, may have all You direct me to give. I hold nothing back. I want all of you. Have Your way, my Love.*

- *How should I give to the keepers of the vineyard?*

- *"You who dwell in the gardens, the companions listen for your voice - Let me hear it!" Song of Solomon 8:13*

- *When I was a fragile, young dove, You wooed me with these Words: "O my dove, in the clefts of the rock, in the secret places of the cliff, let me see your face, let me hear your voice; for your voice is sweet, and your face is lovely." Song of Solomon 2:14*

- *And You embraced me in the secret places of the cliff, until I ceased shivering; You cradled my beating heart in nail-scarred hands, and lifted my fearful face to the flame of love in Your eyes. I came to life on the day I became Yours. I harmonized that which You sang over me. I couldn't believe You wanted to hear my voice! It had mocked You and praised Your enemy, but the wine of Your Word washed over it, and Your honey kisses made it sweet to You.*

- *You who dwell in the gardens, our ears are tuned to Your Song. Let me hear Your voice afresh - cold as the north wind or warm in its comfort - breath of life, breathe on us...*

- *Speak, Lord, we are listening...*

- *"Make haste, my beloved, and be like a gazelle or a young stag on the mountains of spices." Song of Solomon 8:14*

- *Never again the mountains of separation, of leopards, or even of myrrh and aloes. It is done! On the mountain of Your completed victory, as the High Priest of Heaven, make haste in the fragrance of our prayers.*

- *As we longed for Your first kiss, we now long for Your return...our faces are toward You.*

DAY 30 : EMBRACE ME, ETERNITY

And the Spirit and the bride say, 'Come!'
And let him who hears say, 'Come!'
And let him who thirsts come.
Whoever desires, let him take the water of life freely.
(Revelation 22:17)

Embrace me, Eternity
Let Your horizon expand within me.
Melt the chains of my inner man
Keeping me locked from the Promised Land
Where I am created to be.

Flee from me, Compromise
I no more accept your disguise,
Prison of triviality,
Wrapping me in mediocrity,
Choking the truth in fears from lies.

Heavenly freedom, explode.
Lift me into the dimensions You've told
Will unite Your eternal breath
With mine, as I resurrect from death
And the beauty of You unfolds…

(ENDNOTES)

1   http://christian-quotes.ochristian.com/
     Charles-H.-Brent-Quotes/.

2   *Thompson Chain Reference Study Bible,* compiled and edited
     by Frank Charles Thompson, D.D., Ph. D. (Thomas Nelson
     Bibles, 1997), 2069.

3   http://christianquotes.ochristian.com/christianquotes_ochris-
     tian.cgi?query=wine&action=Search&x=0&y=0.

4   Strong's *Hebrew and Greek Dictionaries.* H3196.

5

6   Davidson, Roberts, *Ecclesiastes and the Song of Solomon* 103,
     Saint Andrew Press, Edinburgh, Scotland 1986.
     Deas Vail, *Birds, Birds & Cages* (Brave New World Records,
     2009).

7   C. S. Lewis, *The Lion, The Witch, and The Wardrobe,* (Geoffrey
     Bless, 1950).

8   https://mysacredobsession.wordpress.com/tag/luke/.

9   http://www.abbaoil.com/t-anointingoilteaching.aspx.

10   Robert Jamieson, A.R. Fausset, and David Brown, *Commentary
     Critical and Explanatory on the Whole Bible* 1871.

11   Strong's *Hebrew and Greek Dictionaries.* H4900.

12   Davidson, Robert. *Ecclesiastes and the Song of Solomon.*104. The Saint Andrew Press, Edinburgh, Scotland 1986.

13   Edward T. Welch**. *When People are Big and God is Small*, P&R Publishing, 1997, p. 19. http://www.thegracetabernacle. org/quotes/Fear_of_Man.htm.

14   Strong's *Hebrew and Greek Dictionaries.* H7835.

15   Davidson, Robert. *Ecclesiastes and the Song of Solomon.*105. The Saint Andrew Press, Edinburgh, Scotland 1986.

16   Strong's *Hebrew and Greek Dictionary.* H5046.

17   Ibid. H7257.

18   Ibid. H3303.

19   Ibid. H7462.

20   Gene Edwards, *The Divine Romance* (Tyndale House Publishers, Inc. 1992), 51-52.

21   Page number.

22   http://en.wikipedia.org/wiki/Spikenard.

23   http://www.magi-gifts.com/significance.html.

24   http://www.bibleplaces.com/engedi.htm.

25   Footnote here

26   http://www.brainyquote.com/quotes/keywords/rose.html.

27   http://en.wikipedia.org/wiki/Rose_%28symbolism%29.

28   Robert Jamieson, A.R. Fausset, and David Brown, *Commentary Critical and Explanatory on the Whole Bible* 1871.

29   http://www.theplantexpert.com/springbulbs/LilyoftheValley.html.

30   John Gill, http://www.biblestudytools.com/commentaries/gills-exposition-of-the-bible/song-of-solomon-2-3.html.

31   Strong's *Hebrew and Greek Dictionaries.* H3293.

32   Ibid. H6738.

33   Robert Jamieson, A.R. Fausset, and David Brown, *Commentary Critical and Explanatory on the Whole Bible* 1871.

34   Ibid.

35   Robert Jamieson, A.R. Fausset, and David Brown, *Commentary Critical and Explanatory on the Whole Bible* 1871.

36   Ibid.

37   C.S. Lewis, *Weight of Glory*.

38   http://christianquotes.ochristian.com/christianquotes_ochristian.cgi?query=arise&action=Search&x=0&y=0.

39   Strong's Dictionary.

40   Ibid.

41   Matthew Henry's Concise Commentary.

42   Robert Jamieson, A.R. Fausset, and David Brown, Commentary Critical and Explanatory on the Whole Bible 1871.

43   Strong *Hebrew and Greek Dictionary,* H1336.

44   Strong *Hebrew and Greek Dictionary,* H1335.

45   Gene Edwards, *The Divine Romance,* (Tyndale House Publishers, Inc. 1992), 67.

46   R.C. Sproul. Cosmic Treason, Tabletalk, May 2008, p. 7 http://www.thegracetabernacle.org/quotes/Sin-Love_for.htm.

47   Tim Challies. Escaping Anonymity, Tabletalk, April, 2009, p. 70. http://www.thegracetabernacle.org/quotes/Accountability-Personal.htm.

48   Enhanced Strong's Hebrew and Greek Commentary, H3915.

49   Ibid. H1245.

50   Ibid. H6965.

51   Ibid. H8104.

52   *www.brainyquote.com/quotes/quotes/b/billygraha383246.html.*

53   Kiel-Delitzsch, *Commentary on the Old Testament Vol. 6,* William B. Eermans Publishing Company, 1872, 61.

54   Robert Jamieson, A.R. Fausset, and David Brown*, Commentary Critical and Explanatory on the Whole Bible* 1871.

55   Matthew 16:13-19.

56   Robert Jamieson, A.R. Fausset, and David Brown, *Commentary Critical and Explanatory on the Whole Bible,* 1871.

57   Robert Jamieson, A.R. Fausset, and David Brown, *Commentary Critical and Explanatory on the Whole Bible,* 1871.

58   Ibid.

59   http://www.abundantliving.org/Articles/jesussacrifice.htm.

60   http://www.pbministries.org/books/gill/gills_archive.htm.

61   http://www.pbministries.org/books/gill/Solomons_Song/chapter4/song_04_v07.htm.

62   Lewis, C.S. *Mere Christianity.* http://www.btinternet.com/~a.ghinn/greatsin.htm.

63   http://www.goodreads.com/quotes/show/27076.

64   Pollack, Sarah, CBNnews.com, August 04, 2006.

65   Ibid.

66   Robert Jamieson, A.R. Fausset, and David Brown, *Commentary Critical and Explanatory on the Whole Bible,* 1871.

67   http://thinkexist.com/search/searchquotation.asp?search=garden&page=2.

68   Spurgeon, C.H.

69   Lewis, C. S. *Mere Christianity.* Harper Collins Edition, 2001.

70   Strong's *Hebrew and Greek Dictionaries,* H6315 .

71   http://thinkexist.com/quotes/blaise_pascal/.

72   Strong's *Hebrew and Greek Dictionaries,* H3820.

73   Ibid. H5782.

74   Familiar. Epist. 1.7. ep.1. so Seneca, ep.122.

75   Gill, John, **Weighed in the Balance of God's Word.**

76   Strong's *Hebrew and Greek Dictionaries,* H8535.

77   Gill, John, **Weighed in the Balance of God's Word.**

78   http://www.writespirit.net/authors/mother_teresa/mother_teresa_quotes/mother_teresa_love/.

79   Wiersbe's commentary on 1. John 4 on e-Sword.

80   The Screwtape Letters, Lewis, C.S.

81   Strong's *Hebrew and Greek Dictionaries,* H1993.

82   Ibid. H1245.

83   Ibid. H8104.

84   http://www.brainyquote.com/quotes/authors/c/c_s_lewis.html.

85   Strong's *Hebrew and Greek Dictionaries,* H6703.

86   Robert Jamieson, A.R. Fausset, and David Brown, **Commentary Critical and Explanatory on the Whole Bible,** 1871.

87   Gill, John. *Weighed in the Balance of God's Word.*

88   http://www.thegracetabernacle.org/quotes/Spiritual-Warfare-General.htm.

89   Strong's *Hebrew and Greek Dictionaries,* H7462.

90   Harriet Beecher Stowe, *Uncle Tom's Cabin,* (Dover Publications, Inc. 2005).

91   Erwin W. Lutzer, *When a Nation Forgets God; 7 Lessons We Must Learn from Nazi Germany,* (Moody Publishers, Chicago, 2010), 22.

92   Strong's *Hebrew and Greek Dictionaries,* H366.

93   C. S. Lewis, *The Weight of Glory,* and other addresses.

94   C. S. Lewis, *The Weight of Glory.*

95   http://www.thegracetabernacle.org/quotes/Jesus_Christ-Lordship.htm.

96   http://www.tentmaker.org/Quotes/evangelismquotes.htm.

97   Robert Jamieson, A.R. Fausset, and David Brown, *Commentary Critical and Explanatory on the Whole Bible,* 1871.

98   Francis Chan & Preston Sprinkle, *Erasing Hell,* (David C. Cook Distribution Canada 2011).

99   Robert Jamieson, A.R. Fausset, and David Brown, *Commentary Critical and Explanatory on the Whole Bible,* 1871.

100   Strong's *Hebrew and Greek Dictionaries,* H8326.

101   Ibid. H4197.

102   Ibid. H990.

103   Ron Hansen's foreword in Henri Nouwen's **Can You Drink the Cup?** Ave Maria Press, 1996, 11.

104   Nouwen Henri, **Can You Drink the Cup?** Ave Maria Press, 1996, 122.

105   Thomas Brooks. A Puritan Golden Treasury, compiled by I.D.E. Thomas, by permission of Banner of Truth, Carlisle, PA. 2000, p. 216. http://www.thegracetabernacle.org/quotes/Prayer-Sweetness.htm.

106   Strong's **Hebrew and Greek Dictionaries,** H1295.

107   Robert Jamieson, A.R. Fausset, and David Brown, **Commentary Critical and Explanatory on the Whole Bible,** 1871.

108   Cheyne and Black, **Encyclopedia Biblica** and **Jewish encyclopedia, http://en.wikipedia.org/wiki/Mount_Carmel.**

109   http://thinkexist.com/quotations/sex/.

110   Robert Jamieson, A.R. Fausset, and David Brown, **Commentary Critical and Explanatory on the Whole Bible,** 1871.

111   John Gill, **Exposition on the Book of Solomon's Song.** http://www.pbministries.org/books/gill/Solomons_Song/chapter8/song_08_v01.htm.

112   **Princess Bride**, http://www.imdb.com/title/tt0093779/quotes?qt=qt0482705.

113　Strong's *Hebrew and Greek Dictionaries,* H4057.

114　Ibid. H2048.

115　Ibid. H7514.

116　Strong's *Hebrew and Greek Dictionaries*, H5782.

117　Robert Jamieson, A.R. Fausset, and David Brown, *Commentary Critical and Explanatory on the Whole Bible,* 1871.

118　2 Timothy 2:13.

119　1 Peter 4:8.

120　Lamentations 3:23.

121　John 1:50.

122　Strong's *Hebrew and Greek Dictionaries,* H7843.

123　Deuteronomy 32:5.

124　Exodus 34:6b-7a.

125　Strong's *Hebrew and Greek Dictionaries*, H2368.

126　Exodus 28:11.

127　Isaiah 49:16.

128　Robert Jamieson, A.R. Fausset, and David Brown, *Commentary Critical and Explanatory on the Whole Bible,* 1871.

129　Strong's *Hebrew and Greek Dictionaries*, H5794.

130   Strong's **Hebrew and Greek Dictionaries**, H2346.

131   Ibid. H2905.

132   Ibid. H1802.

133   Luke 18:10.

134   http://www.thegracetabernacle.org/quotes/Jesus_Christ-Lordship.htm.

135   John 21: 15-17.

136   Strong's **Hebrew and Greek Dictionaries,** H1174.

137   Brouillet, Monique Seefried, ed. From Hannibal to Saint Augustine: Ancient Art of North Africa from the Musee du Louvre. Michael C. Carlos Museum, Emory University: Atlanta GA, 1994.

138   Robert Jamieson, A.R. Fausset, and David Brown**, Commentary Critical and Explanatory on the Whole Bible,** 1871.

139   http://www.luther.de/.

140   http://dailychristianquote.com/dcqgraham.html.

141   Ibid.

Made in the USA
Middletown, DE
27 October 2020